WATERSIDE WALKS
In Middlesex &
West London

David Hall & Rosemary Hall

COUNTRYSIDE BOOKS
NEWBURY, BERKSHIRE

COUNTRYSIDE BOOKS
3 Catherine Road
Newbury, Berkshire

ISBN 1 85306 629 X

To view our complete range of books,
please visit us at
www.countrysidebooks.co.uk

Designed by Graham Whiteman
Cover illustration by Colin Doggett
Maps by Rosemary Hall and redrawn by Gelder design & mapping
Photographs by the authors

Produced through MRM Associates Ltd., Reading
Printed by J. W. Arrowsmith Ltd., Bristol

Contents

Area Map Showing Location of the Walks

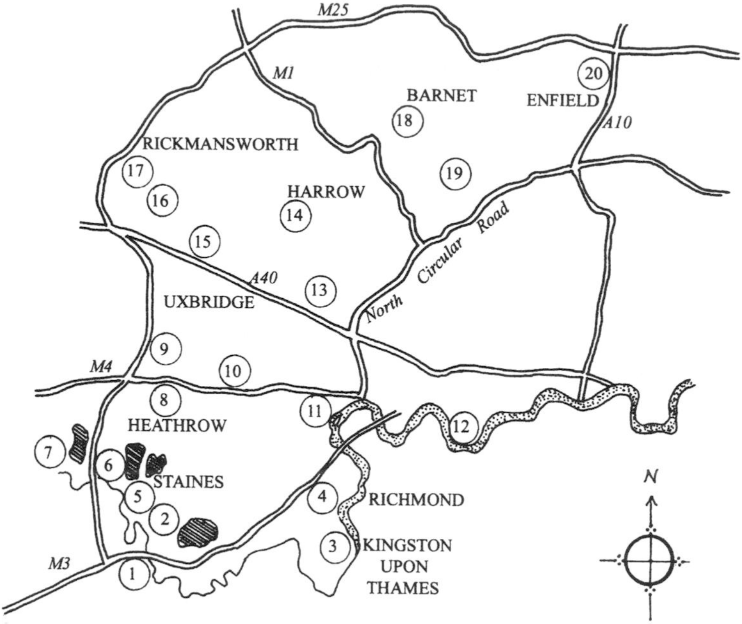

M25

M1

BARNET
⑱

⑳
ENFIELD
A10

RICKMANSWORTH
⑰
⑯

HARROW
⑭

⑲

⑮

A40
⑬
North Circular Road

UXBRIDGE

⑨

M4
⑩

⑧
HEATHROW

⑪
⑫

⑦
⑥
STAINES

⑤

⑯

④
RICHMOND

③
KINGSTON
UPON
THAMES

M3
①

N

Walk

To Our Parents

Publisher's Note

We hope that you obtain considerable enjoyment from this book; great care has been taken in its preparation. Although at the time of publication all routes followed public rights of way or permitted paths, diversion orders can be made and permissions withdrawn.

We cannot, of course, be held responsible for such diversion orders and any inaccuracies in the text which result from these or any other changes to the routes nor any damage which might result from walkers trespassing on private property. We are anxious though that all details covering the walks are kept up to date and would therefore welcome information from readers which would be relevant to future editions.

INTRODUCTION

The Thames is London's countryside. Life of all sorts thrives in, on and beside the river.

These walks lead you past parts of the Thames in outlying areas where it is still natural, such as near the rich alluvial meadows of Staines Moor, to the most famous section, the route of the annual University Boat Race starting in much more urbanised Putney. Even here, in addition to historical buildings and the fine riverscape, you can marvel at the variety of birds that thrive by the river.

West London and Middlesex contain much more than the Thames. You will see where the Colne Brook and River Colne meet the Thames, and walk beside the Brent, Crane, Ash, Pinn and a number of brooks and streams. Many of these minor rivers flow through parks and nature reserves, where you may encounter small mammals such as voles and foxes, and even deer.

Bygone industry has left a landscape now occupied by a variety of wildlife. Some of the watercourses are artificial. These were built either to power mills, such as the Duke of Northumberland's River (you will see its beginning and end), or the Frays River, or simply to supply water, such as the New River and the Longford River. Canals are now a green corridor lined with overgrown banks. They provide perches for waterfowl that compete with each other and lines of patient human anglers for the fish. Gravel extraction has studded the area with lakes that are havens for a host of wildfowl.

In what is now the Crane Park, gunpowder works kept away other activity, and the area around the Shot Tower is now a successful wildlife park. Green spaces are eaten up by human settlements, but unsettled humans whizzing about in cars don't seem to bother fish and other wildlife too much. Some very picturesque routes follow streams that now flow alongside busy roads and motorways.

All of the walks recommend a good pub that will provide food on most days of the week – telephone ahead if you're relying on food. Don't give walkers a bad name by striding into pubs in muddy boots, nursing a half-pint and surreptitiously trying to eat your own sandwiches. Our pubs are meant to be enjoyed. Always ask before leaving your car in a pub car park before walking – many busy places frown on this, and parking is usually available nearby. We travelled to the start of each walk by public transport, and details are given for all routes.

A sketch map accompanies each walk description but you are recommended to carry with you the appropriate Ordnance Survey maps for the area. These are particularly useful for identifying the main features of views. All of the walks are on a set of four Ordnance Survey 1:25 000 scale Explorer maps. These are 160, Windsor, Weybridge and Bracknell; 161, London South (Westminster, Greenwich, Croydon, Esher and Twickenham); 172, Chiltern Hills East (High Wycombe, Maidenhead and Rickmansworth, 173, London North (The City, West End, Enfield, Ealing, Harrow and Watford). Some people prefer to use a street atlas, such as a Nicholson or A to Z atlas – get a copy in colour with as large a coverage as possible.

Walks by water can be very muddy, and water can be a danger for children. They will however be fascinated by the wildlife; take your binoculars to enjoy the walks to the full.

Thanks to everyone who smoothed our path, especially Rachael Hill, Conservation Officer of the Environment Agency for the opening line of this introduction, staff at the pubs, always helpful walkers along the way, and the ever patient people at Countryside Books. David would like to thank Janet Wright for helping with the onerous research and writing up.

We had a lot of pleasure walking these routes – walking by water is special. Some walks give you the extra treat of water on both sides, which is magical. Have fun.

David Hall and Rosemary Hall

LALEHAM: TWO RIVERS
AND THREE LAKES

Starting from the centre of the old village of Laleham, the walk at first follows the Thames Path past some delightful scenery and Chertsey Lock. Then you take a much quieter path between two gravel pit lakes, a haven for wildfowl, before walking along the River Ash next to Shepperton Film Studios.

Chertsey Bridge

Laleham has connections with royalty, nobility and the world of show business. It is also on a prime piece of the Thames. You start off alongside Laleham Park, an expanse of meadow and fine trees that once surrounded the family home of the Earls of Lucan (now private residences). The Thames Path continues past tree-lined banks to Chertsey Lock, usually past a number of anglers after perch, roach, gudgeon and the very rare bream. After a water meadow at Chertsey, a little-used footpath leads between water on both sides, always a magical experience. Then you follow the River Ash for a while.

Shepperton Studios, which you pass, was originally a private estate, and was developed into internationally famous studios between the wars. Parts of the classic *The African Queen* were shot here – but you won't have to wade through tropical rivers on this walk.

Laleham has a number of good pubs, but the Three Horseshoes on Shepperton Road is a very picturesque old coaching inn justly renowned for its food. Get here early as it can get full for lunch, despite the number of bars, lovely large garden and separate restaurant in which to enjoy anything from a snack to a three-course meal. Lunches are available seven days a week from 12 noon to 2.30 pm; evening meals on Monday to Saturday from 6 pm to 9 pm (9.30 pm on Friday and Saturday). The pub keeps all-day opening hours, serves four draught ales including London Pride, Courage Best and Old Speckled Hen and, to keep up the show business connections, Edward VII is said to have had meetings with Lilly Langtry here. Telephone: 01784 452617.

- **HOW TO GET THERE:** Laleham is on the B376 between Shepperton and Staines. Rail: Shepperton and Chertsey stations are both near parts of the walk. Bus services run from both.
- **PARKING:** Near the river, at Laleham Park.
- **LENGTH OF THE WALK:** 6½ miles. Map: OS Explorer 160 (GR 052688).

THE WALK

1. Leave the pub and go down Ferry Lane opposite. As the road veers to the left, pass a large house on the corner, the site of the first prep school in the country, set up by Thomas Arnold's brother-in-law. Follow the right-hand road towards the river. Pass the traffic sign 'wild fowl' – a host of Canada geese seem to have displaced the swans here – and turn left onto the Thames Path. On your left the paddock is followed by Laleham Park and the car park. On the right is a grass verge and shallow bank to the river, lined by a profusion of willows. As the riverside narrows, follow the gravel path. On the right is a reservoir embankment. The grass verge reappears; pass the entrance to Laleham Park and a campsite and a car park (next to a toilet block and café). Pass the play and picnic areas, then, just visible on the left, is the surface of a gravel pit lake; the whole area is a wildfowl haven. Pass the entrance to Spelthorne Barefoot Waterski Club on the left. After an attractive line of poplars on the opposite bank go under the M3 bridge.

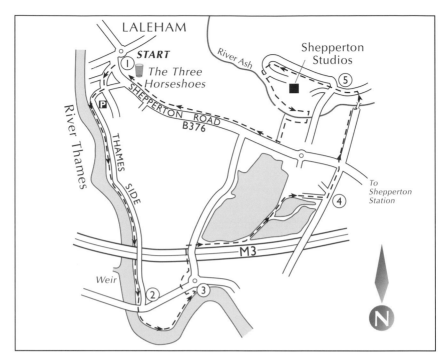

Continue on to the weir and Chertsey Lock. The house on the left by the lock is adorned by circular paintings. Continue towards the bridge right beside the river.

2. Stay on the footpath underneath the busy road bridge. Enter Chertsey Meadow through the wooden kissing gate. This is a water meadow with occasional riverbank tree and a natural shallow bank into the river. Pass on the right the entrance to a marina; on the left are extensive meadows. A small metal post in the ground bears the arms of the City of London and is inscribed 'Conservators of the River Thames'. On the right is a boatyard, then a picnic area, contrasting with the natural meadow on this side. The river bank here has many small sandy 'beaches' sloping down to shallow water. On the left near a pylon is a sunken boggy area full of grasses and willows – a watering hole for the cattle.

3. At the end of the meadow, do not go through the kissing gate; turn left by the fence, follow the public footpath sign and leave the meadow by the stile onto the road. Turn right, then at the roundabout turn left onto Littleton Lane. Cross the M3 bridge. At the other side immediately turn right onto the public footpath and walk down towards the gravel pit lakes. Follow the path down to the motorway fence and walk past the boat club on the left at the end of the lake. Go through a gate – the path from here may be muddy and overgrown – and very shortly after, turn left onto a public footpath through the wooden fence over plank bridges. You are now on a thin spit of land lined by trees and undergrowth between two lakes, with occasional spots for anglers. Despite the noise from the M3, the right-hand lake is a relatively undisturbed haven for waterfowl; you may see herons. The lake on the left is used for sailing. Keep straight on across a concrete footbridge. At the end of the lake on the right cross a bridge and turn right at the signpost marked 'Sheep Walk'. Follow this path along the north shore of the lake, now on your right-hand side; cross a stile then after a few houses turn left at the road – Sheep Walk.

4. Pass Shepperton Methodist Church. Go across the crossroads, following Watersplash Road. Behind the houses on the right are gravel pit ponds, attracting wildfowl. Watersplash Road now reveals the secret of its name: at the River Ash it ends in a ford, which has been barred to vehicles since the M3 was built. As you cross the footbridge, look for two swans that are regulars and for kingfishers perching on willows and shrubs. Continue along the path and turn left onto Squires Bridge Road.

5. Turn right onto Studios Road, walk past Shepperton Studios, follow the road round to the left past stores and a bus stop, then turn into Wilcox Gardens and walk down to the river. Turn left and follow this pleasant riverside walk through trees. Studio buildings you pass on the left include the Korda Theatre, the David Lean Building and the former manor house of the estate that is now the studios. As you approach the road, notice in the river a piece of statuary which predates the film studios. Leave the riverside walk through the gateway, turn right and cross the bridge over the Ash. Take the first right into the recreation ground and walk along the river bank. Turn left at the end and walk down to Laleham Road. Turn right and walk back into Laleham to return to the pub.

PLACES OF INTEREST NEARBY
Chertsey, just the other side of the river, is an interesting historical town with the site of an old abbey, the fine Old Town Hall and a museum which is open on Tuesday to Friday from 12.30 pm to 4.30 pm and on Saturday from 11 am to 4 pm (free admission).

THE THAMES BETWEEN LALEHAM
AND STAINES

Firstly you pass by some green corridors alongside gravel pits and minor rivers, and walk over common land into Staines. The walk then follows some fine riverside along the Thames Path, and shows you a marvellous wildlife reserve on an island in the river.

The River Thames at Staines

Laleham is perhaps most famous for its association with the Binghams, the family name of the Earls of Lucan. Their home was here, and the family tomb is in the churchyard. Another of Laleham's famous family names is Arnold. Thomas, the famous headmaster of Rugby School, began his career here, and the playing field of Matthew Arnold School, named after his son, lies close to the walk. The community spirit of the village is reflected in the recent restoration of a village pond as a wildlife resource.

You walk into Staines alongside gravel pit lakes next to the giant

Queen Mary Reservoir, then follow the line of the River Ash and a minor stream, before taking the Thames Path. You pass some very pleasant riverside scenes — swans can often be seen here — along a path lined by many trees, especially willows, and anglers after perch. Much of the river bank is tamed by pilings, but there are natural sections sloping down to shallow water. The walk includes a real treasure – Penton Hook Island, an important wildlife reserve, with a rich mixture of trees, grasses and wet areas attracting a wide variety of songbirds, sparrowhawks and kingfishers.

Laleham has a number of good pubs. This walk starts at the Feathers, a popular pub on The Broadway that keeps all-day opening hours seven days a week. There is a large, comfortable bar at the front furnished with settles and small tables, and a separate eating area partitioned off by a half-height wall surmounted by old sewing machines. A changing range of beers is served from hand pumps, and food is available every day until about 9.30 pm. One unusual feature is that fish and chips are also available as a takeaway. Families are welcomed. Telephone: 01784 453561.

- **HOW TO GET THERE:** Laleham is on the B376 Staines-Shepperton road, and The Broadway, the B377 from Ashford, joins this in the centre of the village. Rail: The walk passes very close to Staines station (Reading-Waterloo line).
- **PARKING:** There are car parks in the nearby riverside Laleham Park.
- **LENGTH OF THE WALK:** 6 miles. Map: OS Explorer 160 (GR 053690).

THE WALK

1. Leave the pub, and turn right onto The Broadway. Just before the water channel, on the right is the recently restored Laleham Pond, which is occasionally open to the public (contact Spelthorne Borough Council on 01784 446339). Cross over the water channel by the pumping station. Cross the road to take the path on the left-hand side (not the signposted footpath off to the left). The woodland on the right is full of bird and insect life despite the busy road. The recreation ground on the left is near the Matthew Arnold School. Cross the bridge over the reservoir aqueduct and come to the roundabout. Cross the busy Kingston Road, turn right, go under power lines, then turn left into Fordbridge Park.

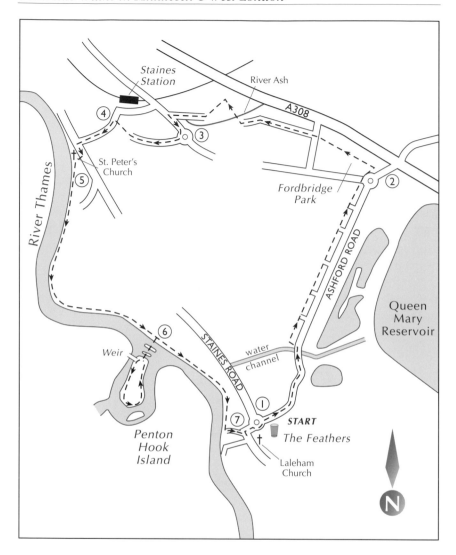

2. Take the tarmac path under the power lines then turn right onto the path down the avenue. Continue between the trees, roughly following the line of pylons. Exit the park via the tarmac path through the gate on the left-hand end (without going under the flyover). Cross the road, turn right, then turn left almost straight away into Brookside Avenue. Follow this to the end into Boundary Road. Follow Boundary Road under power cables, then round to the right. Walk in the direction of the pylon in the field to the end of the road and turn left onto the footpath at the fence. Behind the fence on the right is the River Ash. Take the footbridge over the aqueduct, then turn right, with the Ash now on your left. Go through a kissing gate (possibly vandalised) and enter Shortwood Common. Stay on the path to the right of this natural common land following the fenced-off aqueduct on the right. Go through an open gateway in the hedge, then take a path to the half-left through this part of the common, meeting a vehicle track from the right. Continue along this, as it veers round to the right and becomes a proper road. This rejoins the Ash, then veers to the left to join the main road.

3. Cross straight over the busy road with care to go down Knowle Green, passing between civic offices on the right and law courts on the left, then passing the leisure centre. Continue along this road, which is blocked off to vehicles and then becomes a tree-lined path.

4. Turn left away from the railway station onto Gresham Road, which has pleasant older houses behind leafy gardens. At the end turn left onto the main Laleham Road. Cross the road at the Victorian red brick church – St Peter's – then go through the churchyard on the left of the church, passing a cedar tree. Just to the right of the lychgate is a small memorial garden to the Burma Campaign.

5. Leave the churchyard to the left of the lychgate and turn left onto the Thames towpath. Pass moorings and then cross the small bridge over a stream whose overgrown banks are a green corridor. Grassland and large mature trees on the left belong to a private garden. On the Surrey side of the river you will see the headquarters and watchtower of Staines Sailing Club. Pass a picnic area on the right. Enter a broad sweep of meadow; the path is on the left, but, if the ground is dry enough, walk by the river. Willow roots poke out into the water, and there are little 'sandy' beaches where erosion is encroaching on the meadow. Amongst other wildlife, sheltering under a stone you may find a small crab – Chinese mitten crabs, an inadvertent import, are thriving in the Thames. Return to the path as the meadow narrows. Pass a public footpath sign (1 mile to Laleham) and more moorings. You can see a lock in the near distance. Cross a plank bridge, then pass a line of poplars. Pass the end of a lane and another footpath sign (still 1 mile to Laleham!).

6. At Penton Hook Lock, explore Penton Hook Island wildlife reserve. Cross the footbridge on closed lock gates and continue over the weir. The island was formed when the first lock was built in 1815. Spoil from dredging in the 1940s was spread over the island, so all the plantlife dates from then. Enter the island on the north side via the next bridge over the overspill weir. To the right is the gauge weir on the main river channel. Take the path crossing the new fish-spawning channel and come down the right-hand side to the southern bank, which hosts the uncommon yellow brimstone butterfly. Pass a picnic area, and return via the wetlands, connected to the river by footbridges. Return via the lock gates to the Thames Path and turn right. Pass the Thames Water site (Laleham Raw Water Intake). Keep to the riverside path as the road turns away to the left (opposite Laleham Boat Yard).

7. Opposite Harris Boatbuilders turn left onto Blacksmiths Lane (signposted 'Local Shops'). Pass the Old Forge and Forge Cottage and then the war memorial at the end. Cross the busy road, turn left and pass Laleham church. Continue along The Broadway to return to the pub.

PLACES OF INTEREST NEARBY
The churchyard of *Laleham church* has the Lucan family tomb. The 3rd earl, who ordered the Charge of the Light Brigade, is buried here (but not the 7th, who is still missing). Matthew Arnold, the poet and Oxford academic born in Laleham, also lies here.

TEDDINGTON, BUSHY PARK AND THE RIVER THAMES

Starting along traditional Teddington High Street, you pass shops selling antiques, books, furniture and bric-a-brac, and restaurants and coffee shops   and not a supermarket in sight. The route proceeds to Bushy Park where imposing avenues, sweeping grasslands and grazing deer contrast with the Woodland Gardens where a variety of waterfowl inhabit the ponds. You then pass the Diana Fountain and the Bushy Park ponds and end the walk along a pleasant section of the Thames Path.

Teddington Bridge

Early on the walk you pass the parish church of St Mary with St Alban where the notorious Peg Woffington (1714-1760), an Irish actress who also appeared frequently on the London stage, is buried. She spent her last years as a semi-invalid in Teddington, and the cottage that is now the old-world Peg Woffington Tea Rooms was reputedly owned by her.

Bushy Park is a royal park which was opened to the public in 1838.

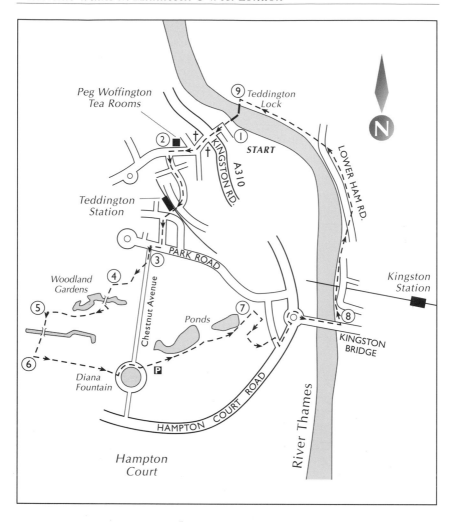

Bushy House was built in the late 17th century, altered greatly in the 18th century, and was the home of the Park Ranger. Before he became King, William IV lived there with his mistress and after he died in 1837, his widow Queen Adelaide used it. The house is now the headquarters of the National Physical Laboratory (NPL), the most important aspect of whose work is metrology, the science of weights and measures, and includes establishing standards, methods of measurement and calibration tests. There is no public access to the house or its gardens but the walk continues through Bushy Park and past its marvellous ponds.

A pub boasting a French chef on its outside board has quite a reputation to live up to, and the Tide End Cottage pub in Ferry Road, Teddington, succeeds in doing this. As well as tasty pub fare, more unusual dishes are on offer such as rabbit with tarragon pie, lobster, and beef and Guinness pie. Beers on draught include Greene King IPA, Abbot Ale and John Smith's Bitter. Food is served on Monday to Saturday from 12 noon to 2.30 pm and 6 pm to 9.30 pm and on Sunday from 12 noon to 5 pm. Telephone: 020 8892 0863.

- **HOW TO GET THERE:** Take the A310 to Teddington. Turn towards the river down Ferry Road to find Tide End Cottage on the right. Rail: Teddington station (trains from Waterloo) is near the beginning of the walk.
- **PARKING:** In Bushy Park there are car parks just south east of Bushy House and near the Diana Fountain.
- **LENGTH OF THE WALK:** 5 miles. Map: OS Explorer 161 (GR 167714).

THE WALK

1. From the pub turn left and walk along Ferry Road. Cross Kingston Road and continue ahead, passing the former St Alban's church which now houses the Landmark Arts Centre; opposite is the parish church of St Mary with St Alban. Pass the Peg Woffington Tea Rooms a little further along on the right, and continue ahead along the High Street.

2. Turn left at Cedar Road, cross over Bridgeman Road and walk along Blackmores Grove. Cross Cromwell Road and then the footbridge over the railway line. At the T-junction turn left and go along the alleyway. Cross Clarence Road and continue ahead along Avenue Road. Turn right onto Park Road, and cross over at the zebra crossing to turn left into Bushy Park.

3. Veer right onto a dirt track and continue ahead, passing a sports ground, beyond which is Bushy House. Cross over Cobbler's Walk and turn right onto the footpath running parallel to it. At the T-junction turn left and continue ahead along the tarmac.

4. Opposite a disabled parking bay, enter the Woodland Gardens (open 9 am to dusk, no dogs allowed) through the gate on the left. The fence protects the gardens from deer. Go straight ahead, cross the wooden footbridge over the stream and continue ahead. At the T-junction turn right to walk by the pond and then continue ahead along this path.

5. Leave the park through the wooden gate, walk ahead to the T-junction, turn left and proceed ahead to cross Red Brick Bridge and continue to the next T-junction.

6. Turn left, continue to the Diana Fountain, cross the road and turn left to walk on the grass around the lake. After passing the end of Chestnut Avenue, turn left to walk across the car park. Continue ahead, walking to the right of the Boating Pool and Heron Pond. At the bridge at the top of the Heron Pond, turn right and proceed to the Leg of Mutton Pond. At the top of this pond cross the footbridge, and at the T-junction turn right onto Cobbler's Walk.

7. Just before Hampton Wick Gate turn right and continue ahead, keeping on the path as it turns right. Turn left and then left again to skirt a sports field. Continue ahead, go through a metal gate and walk along the narrow Chestnut Avenue. At Church Grove turn right; at the T-junction turn left onto Hampton Court Road, and follow the road to the White Hart pub. Cross Upper Teddington High Street and go over Kingston Bridge.

8. Turn left by the sign for the Royal Barge bar, and then right to descend the steps to the river. Turn right at the river, and after skirting around the Slug and Lettuce pub, go under the railway bridge. Cross Down Hall Road and continue ahead along Barge Walk, between parkland and the river. When the track ends continue along Lower Ham Road. When the road veers inland, go ahead along the track nearest to the river.

9. Cross the bridge at Teddington Lock, one of 45 locks on the river and the last one before the tidal Thames. Continue ahead along Ferry Road to return to the pub.

PLACES OF INTEREST NEARBY

Hampton Court Palace is the largest and most impressive of the riverside royal palaces. The grounds consist of delightful formal gardens with the famous maze. If you wish to visit the palace while on the walk, turn right at the Diana Fountain and proceed along the southern section of Chestnut Avenue to leave the park by Hampton Court Gate. Telephone: 020 8781 9500.

TWICKENHAM AND THE RIVER CRANE

This pretty linear walk starts by the Thames opposite Eel Pie Island. The route then follows the River Crane through park and woodland, taking in two nature reserves along the way. It continues through Hanworth Park to Feltham station, whence you return to Twickenham by train.

The River Crane

Eel Pie Island derives its name from Victorian times when a tavern there sold eel pies to daytrippers who came by boat from London. The pies and the tavern are no more, the latter ending its days as a hippy squat in the 60s. The Rolling Stones, amongst others, played there then. Things have quietened down considerably, although the colourful Trevor Baylis, the inventor, now lives there. The two main paths on the island are both cul-de-sacs, making a circular walk of the island impossible.

Walking along the bank of the River Crane you pass a tall brick tower, known locally as the Shot Tower. The river once fed watermills used in gunpowder mills built on the adjacent island in the 18th century and closed in 1926. The tower would have been a water and firewatch tower – the mills suffered 55 explosions altogether. The dangers of living near such an industry hampered urban development, with the result that much of the natural landscape remains, comprising a wild habitat of grassland, trees and bushes as a green corridor.

Opposite the tower is the Crane Park Island Nature Reserve. Here, and on the river bank, a variety of broad-leaved trees grow. The route continues along the river to the Pevensey Road Local Nature Reserve, a habitat for many species of wildflowers, insects and small mammals, as well as numerous birds. In summer the humming insects almost drown out the distant noise of traffic.

The walk starts at a pub which was established in 1727 as the Queen's Head but over the years came to be known as the 'Barmy Arms', and locals will tell you that this name referred to one of the early landlords who was renowned for his barminess. The mundane explanation that it referred to the froth on the top of fermenting ale is more likely, 'barmy' being an old name for frothy.

There are a number of tables outside where you can eat peacefully facing the river (The Embankment is pedestrianised) and the pub has a separate restaurant, where children are welcome – they are not allowed in the bar. The Barmy Arms is open all day and food is served from 11 am to 9.30 pm on Monday to Saturday and from 12 noon to 9 pm on Sunday. A large choice of main courses is available as well as snacks, and the draught beers include Courage Best, Directors and Abbot. Telephone: 020 8892 0863.

- **HOW TO GET THERE:** The pub is on The Embankment at Twickenham, reached on the A305 from Richmond. Rail: Twickenham station. The walk ends at Feltham, three stations west on the same line.
- **PARKING:** There is a public car park in front of the pub accessible from King Street via Water Lane. Hourly charge; free on Sundays and public holidays.
- **LENGTH OF THE WALK:** 4½ miles. Map: OS Explorer 161 (GR 164732).

THE WALK

1. Leave the pub, turn left and then left again to walk along Church Lane, passing the church of St Mary-the-Virgin on the right. Follow the road as it bends left (now Arragon Road), cross over York Street and continue ahead. At the T-junction turn right onto London Road. Continue ahead across the bridge and past Twickenham station. At the three-ways junction, continue ahead along Whitton Road.

2. Turn left onto Court Way, and left again onto Craneford Way. Continue to the end and turn left onto the cycle path, signposted 'River Crane Walk'. Continue ahead with the railway line on your left. At the T-junction turn left onto a cycle path, signposted 'Whitton'. At the path's end continue along the cement road and cross the bridge over the River Crane. Turn right onto Mereway Road, cross the footbridge and turn left onto the tarmac path in Kneller Gardens that runs alongside the river. Walk through this pleasant park, then cross Meadway and continue ahead along the wide tarmac path, bearing left at the fork to stay near the river. Pass a playing field on the right, then go under the bridge at Hospital Bridge Road and, soon after, Great Chertsey Road bridge (A316). Continue ahead by the river, following a signpost for Feltham. This is a pretty, tree-fringed stretch of the river.

3. Where the main tarmac track veers right, continue ahead on the narrow dirt track through a line of trees to the Shot Tower, on the right. Just after the tower, turn left, go through the metal gates and cross the bridge to enter the Crane Park Island Nature Reserve. Cross a second bridge and veer right to keep on the main path. After crossing two more bridges veer left at the fork, and continue ahead along a path which skirts the left river bank. When the main path turns right, turn left, descend the wooden steps and continue along a narrow path that runs close to the river. Continue ahead and ascend the wooden steps. Turn left, leave the reserve by the gates you entered, and turn left to continue through woodland along the path closest to the river.

4. At the T-junction veer left and continue ahead on the wide tarmac path to Hounslow Road. Turn left here and continue ahead to cross two bridges.

5. Immediately after the second bridge, turn right and cross the road via the traffic island, to enter the Pevensey Road Local Nature Reserve;

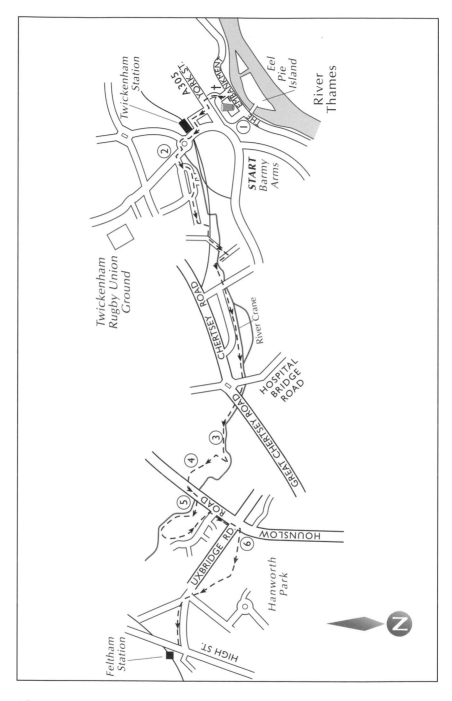

walk along the path on the left side of the river. Continue ahead following a yellow arrow and at the fork veer right to go down wooden steps. At the T-junction, where the river veers right and goes under a bridge, turn left to go slightly uphill. Keep on this main path, crossing straight over the crosspaths. You are now in open, pleasant meadow dotted with trees. Continue ahead to the end of the path and go through the metal kissing gate onto Pevensey Road.

Turn left and walk to Hounslow Road. Turn right and continue ahead. Cross Uxbridge Road and walk to Hanworth Park on the right. Turn right through the gate to enter the park. Continue ahead on the narrow path across the grass. Turn right onto the wide gravel track and continue ahead passing a sports ground on the left and a children's playground on the right. At the end of the path veer right onto a narrow path running to the right of the Longford River.

6. A short way along look for the end of a fenced off tree plantation across the grass on the right. Turn right and continue ahead with the plantation on your right and Feltham Community School sports field on your left. At the end of the sports field turn left and continue ahead keeping the sports fields on your left. Follow the path as it veers right and leave the park. Turn left on Uxbridge Road, cross Browells Lane and veer left onto Hanworth Road and continue ahead to the High Street, Feltham. Cross over to enter Feltham station.

PLACES OF INTEREST NEARBY

Orleans House Gallery, Riverside, Twickenham (turn left from the pub, along the river) shows changing exhibitions and paintings of 18th and 19th century Richmond. Open in the afternoons, Tuesday to Saturday and bank holidays; entry is free. Telephone: 020 8892 0221.

Rugby fans may prefer to visit the *Museum of Rugby* at the Rugby Football Union Ground in Rugby Road. For opening details telephone: 020 8892 8877.

WALK 5

STAINES RESERVOIRS AND BEDFONT LAKES COUNTRY PARK

On this varied walk you take a path between two reservoirs, giving you the unusual experience of looking down on large bodies of water on either side. You continue along a path by the Longford River before exploring one of the most diverse and valuable wildlife reserves within the Greater London area.

The Bedfont Lakes Country Park

Bedfont Lakes Country Park, to the east of Staines, is a fascinating place to visit at any time of year. It consists of a number of important ecological habitats which support a wide range of plants, birds (over 100 species have been recorded) and animals. In addition, the grassland of the park attracts many insects, particularly butterflies, and in summer colourful dragonflies hover over the lakes.

The Old Red Lion where the walk begins is a cosy traditional pub overlooking a tranquil green on the outskirts of Staines. Tasty, well-

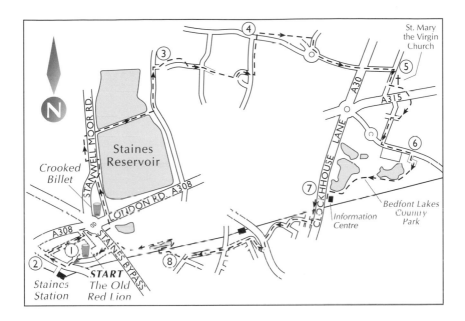

prepared meals and snacks, ranging from fisherman's platter to jacket potatoes, are available on Monday to Saturday (no food on Sunday) from 12 noon to 2.30 pm. Food is not served in the evenings. Draught beers include Courage Best and Fuller's London Pride. Children accompanied by adults are allowed in the garden which overlooks the green, but not inside the pub. Telephone: 01784 453355.

- **HOW TO GET THERE:** Approaching from London, Staines is reached on the A30, then the A308. Turn south into Kingston Road, then left into Leacroft. The Old Red Lion is on the left. Rail: Staines station is nearby (Reading to Waterloo line).
- **PARKING:** On the pub forecourt (please ask before leaving your car whilst you walk) and at weekends on the road. There are car parks at both entrances to Bedfont Lakes Country Park.
- **LENGTH OF THE WALK:** 10 miles. Map: OS Explorer 160 (GR 044715).

THE WALK

1. Leave the pub, turn right and continue along Leacroft to the T-junction with Kingston Road. Turn right and continue ahead passing the approach road to Staines station on the left.

2. Turn right onto Sidney Road, continue ahead and at the T-junction turn left onto Greenlands Road and then right onto London Road. Follow the road around to cross the footbridge over the Staines Bypass (A308) and continue along the A30, passing the Crooked Billet pub on the left. At the pedestrian lights, cross over and go straight ahead along Stanwell New Road, maintaining direction when it merges into Stanwell Moor Road. When the pavement ends, cross the road with care to continue along the pavement on the left side. Cross back over to turn right through the kissing gate at the Thames Water sign into the grounds of the Staines Reservoirs, signposted 'Stanwell 1 mile'. This path leads you straight between the two reservoirs. All too soon you come down to Town Lane where you turn left and continue ahead.

3. Turn right onto Lord Knyvett Close and walk to St Mary the Virgin, Stanwell parish church. Enter the grounds by the lychgate and veer left to reach the porch. Walk from here towards the main gate, but turn right onto a tarmac path just before it to leave the grounds by a smaller metal gate. At the fork veer slightly left and continue ahead. At the next fork bear right and at Falcon Drive turn left and continue ahead. Cross over Clare Road and continue ahead on the narrow footpath to the left of the entrance gates to school grounds. Continue ahead along this path, ignoring the turn off to the left. Keep on the path as it veers right and then left over a footbridge. Continue along the path when it veers left and at the end turn right onto Clay Lane. At the T-junction with Long Lane, turn left, cross the road and continue ahead.

4. Turn right onto Bedfont Road and almost immediately, crossing the road with care, turn left and cross the footbridge. Then turn right onto a grassy path between the two strips of the Longford River. Continue ahead to Beacon Road, cross over with care and turn right to walk to the roundabout. Veer left and then turn left onto Stanwell Road. Continue along here to the A30. Cross at the lights to continue ahead along a quieter section of Stanwell Road.

5. At the T-junction turn right onto Hatton Road, cross over the road and maintain direction to the attractive church of St Mary the Virgin which overlooks Bedfont Green. With your back to the church entrance, cross the road and then take the tarmac path across Bedfont Green to Staines Road (A315). Cross this busy road with care and continue ahead on a tarmac track across another stretch of green. At the T-junction veer left onto Bedfont Green Close and keep going to Bedfont Road. Turn left and continue to the Country Park.

6. Turn right to enter the park. Walk straight ahead across the car park and go through the metal barriers. Veer left onto the gravel track and then right to follow it around the lake. Cross the footbridge and at the crosspaths veer right and then immediately left to ascend to the top of the Motte. Facing away from the car park turn right to descend to the perimeter path around the Motte and then descend the wooden steps. Turn left onto the gravel track and continue ahead. At the T-junction veer right and follow the path around to the lake. Veer left, following the sign to the information centre. At the fork veer right and continue ahead to pass close by a lake on the right. At the end of the lake veer right onto a grassy path and go through a wooden gate into a nature reserve. Turn left and continue ahead along the path, to the right of a fence and ditch Continue in the same direction, go through a wooden gate and continue ahead. Turn right onto a wide gravel track and pass close to the lake on the right. Continue on this main path to the information centre. Then turn left and left again to leave the park.

7. Turn left onto Clockhouse Lane. Continue ahead along the pavement and at the 'road narrows' sign, cross over to walk over the bridge on the right side. There is no pavement here so take great care. Turn right into Parkland Road and continue right along Parkland Grove. Turn right at the T-junction into Village Way and follow it around to Church Road. Cross over at the lights, turn right onto Station Road and then left onto Woodthorpe Road and continue ahead.

8. Where the road bends, just after Ashford Sports Club, turn right and continue along the signposted public footpath to Shortwood Common. Cross the footbridge over the railway and turn immediately left onto a tarmac path to the left of a playing field. At the end of the playing field go through the kissing gate and continue across the common. Turn right to go through a kissing gate and through the underpass on the right. Continue along Leacroft, back to the Old Red Lion.

PLACES OF INTEREST NEARBY
The information centre at *Bedfont Lakes Country Park*, passed on the walk, is open every day except Christmas Day from 8 am until dusk or 9 pm, whichever is earlier. Telephone: 01784 423556.

THE THAMES AND COLNE BROOK WEST OF STAINES

This walk includes parts of the surprisingly green Thames Path on both banks, as well as some quieter places by gravel pit lakes and minor rivers in an area relatively free from housing and industry.

The lock seen on the walk

Staines occupies an important position on the Thames, sited at the point where it meets the River Colne, and close to the confluence with Colne Brook. This gives the site a long history. In Roman times the settlement here was known as Ad Pontes, the Latin name referring to bridges in the plural. You will cross two Thames bridges. Staines Bridge, built in 1832, may be rather newer than Roman, but is definitely older than that carrying both the M25 and A30. This is very busy, but gives a good view of the mouth of Colne Brook.

Although human activity in the form of road and rail traffic is inescapable, the walk mostly passes through areas relatively untouched

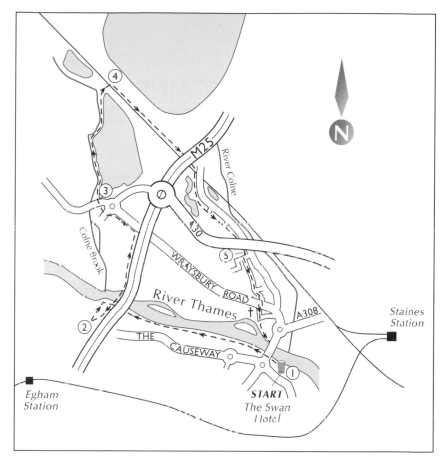

by building. The Thames Path is pleasantly shaded by willow, chestnut and sycamore trees and there is much greenery. You have water on both sides between Colne Brook and a gravel pit lake. This path may be a little overgrown (some nettles in summer), so dress accordingly, but its wildness and position between the waters makes it very rewarding. The gravel pit lakes near the Wraysbury Reservoir attract waterfowl, and the space between is a breeding ground for rabbits especially.

The Swan Hotel, dating from the 15th century, has a wonderful position right by the river – you can usually see swans from the riverside windows. The pub is on The Hythe, next to Staines Bridge, on the south side of the river, technically in Egham, but they proudly give their address as Staines, Middlesex. This is a Fuller's English Inn, so naturally their ever-popular beers are on draught. There is also a

31

wine list. A wide range of good food is available from 12 noon to 10 pm (9.30 pm on Sunday). Blackboards show the house specialities, and there is a printed menu. The beer often features as an ingredient of pies or fish batter. Excellent hot meals, smaller (or larger) sandwiches, vegetarian choices and desserts can be enjoyed in the pleasant riverside dining room, where children are welcome and which has some non-smoking tables. There is also a comfortable riverside bar. Telephone: 01784 452494.

- **HOW TO GET THERE:** Staines is reached on the A30, then the A308, coming west from London. The Hythe is the first left over Staines Bridge. Rail: Staines station (Reading-Waterloo line).
- **PARKING:** There is little street parking in The Hythe. There are quieter streets on the other side of the river off Wraysbury Road, or, a little way up the Thames Path to the west, the car park at Runnymede.
- **LENGTH OF THE WALK:** 4½ miles. Map: OS Explorer 160 (GR 032715).

THE WALK

1. On leaving the pub, take the Thames Path (Surrey side) left towards Staines Bridge. Walk by the attractive 18th century housing in this conservation area, over the small footbridge and continue under the road. Pass moorings – on the opposite side of the river is Church Island, site of plush private homes. Cross a footbridge over a disused basin. The river bank then becomes wilder. Opposite, after the island, is a park, and the view is followed by Holm Island. Both banks have copious tree cover, making for a shady walk. Left of the path, blue railings hide a Thames Water installation. Opposite is a grand building with a long drive. Cross a footbridge over a sidestream, go through a wooded area, then cross a second footbridge. Walk under the bridges carrying the A30 and M25 over the Thames. Turn left onto a gravel path between poplars, and turn left at the road.

2. Cross the river – you get a view of the lock and the junction of Colne Brook and the Thames. On the other side the footpath descends from the roads, becoming wild on each side. Behind the brambles and elder trees to the left is a gravel pit lake. Cross the aqueduct. Turn left at the road, and keep straight on past the homes on the left, bypassing the roundabout to the right. Turn left (towards Wraysbury, B376) and cross over.

3. Just before the bridge (opposite the MOT centre), turn right down steps, signposted 'Colne Valley Park public footpath'. Cross the stile and keep straight on along a narrow bar of land between Colne Brook on the left and a gravel pit lake. Pass angling positions on the left. This is a very green route, passing reeds, sedge and, at times, a lot of nettles! Follow the yellow footpath signs near the power cables at the end of the gravel pit. Cross a stile and, with care, the railway, then turn right.

4. This well-kept fenced path runs between the Wraysbury Reservoir and the railway. The fences keep out people, favouring wildlife, a circumstance exploited by plenty of rabbits. Cross a plank bridge. To the right of the railway is a gravel pit lake. Cross a stile into the meadow as the fence veers to the left – keep by the railway. Follow the overhead power cables to the corner of the field and at the end on the left cross a stile. Keep straight on across a metal stile in a metal fence onto a road. Go under the M25 bridge. Turn right onto a track over the railway bridge (ignore a bicycle track to Staines Moor). Pass a pond, and possibly anglers, on the left, and then the (private) Moor Lane Conservation Area; goats may be in the field. Continue past the Swan Inn and, on the left, the remains of a drinking trough. On the left of the road is the Wraysbury River, with pleasing overgrown banks. Go over a water intake, then under the A30 bridge.

5. Immediately after the bridge, turn right onto a public footpath, then again immediately left to cross the aqueduct. Follow this public footpath across the next road, between trees and the ends of gardens. Keep straight on as the path becomes a road. Pass Duncroft Manor, cross Wraysbury Road and pass St Mary's church. This is an 1828 brick building on a site established by St Erminildus in AD 675. At Church Street, and the pub, turn right, then at the footbridge to Church Island turn left along the riverside walk. Follow the path by some impressive riverside trees to Staines Bridge. From the bridge you can see on the left, just downstream, where the combined River Colne and Wraysbury River join the Thames. Return to The Hythe.

PLACES OF INTEREST NEARBY

The *Old Town Hall* near the river now houses an Arts Centre, and next to it, the Old Fire Station is home to *Spelthorne Museum*, with exhibits on local history and archaeology. Admission is free, and it is open Wednesday, Friday and Saturday afternoons. Telephone: 01784 461084.

STAINES MOOR AND THE WRAYSBURY LAKES

Despite being close to Heathrow Airport and the M25, lakes, rivers, reservoirs and Staines Moor invest this area with a great variety of birds, wildflowers and insects. The walk begins at the picturesque village of Wraysbury from where you take a leafy path by a lake, and then another path between the Wraysbury Reservoir and Colne Brook to reach Staines Moor and the River Colne. After going through a nature reserve to the pleasant village of Horton you return to Wraysbury along a woodland path which passes several of the Wraysbury Lakes.

The Colne Brook

Both the Wraysbury Lakes and Staines Moor are Sites of Special Scientific Interest. The lakes are a habitat for great crested grebes, cormorants, herons, Canada geese and terns. Staines Moor is ancient common land and was designated one of the first SSSIs in the country in 1955.

The Perseverance pub in Wraysbury is where the walk begins. Look at the sign, which depicts a snail crawling to an ark, for a clue as to the origin of its name. The pub has a cosy interior, with wood-beamed ceilings and large open fireplaces. There are two bars, a dining room and a pleasant garden at the rear. As well as tasty bar snacks, special dishes such as whole pheasant with red currant jelly and port and lentil sauce are offered. The beers include Courage Best, Directors, Budweiser and John Smith's. The pub keeps all-day hours, from 11.30 am on Monday to Saturday and from 12 noon on Sunday. Telephone: 01784 482375.

- **HOW TO GET THERE:** Take the A30 to junction 13 of the M25 and continue west along the B376. Turn right along Wraysbury's High Street to reach the Perseverance on the left. Rail: Wraysbury station, just along Station Road to the east (trains from Waterloo).
- **PARKING:** On the pub forecourt, but please ask before leaving your car whilst you walk, or in the car park at Wraysbury station.
- **LENGTH OF THE WALK:** 6½ miles. Map: OS Explorer 160 (GR 006742).

THE WALK

1. On leaving the pub, turn right and walk the short distance to the Wraysbury Baptist Church, which was built in 1840 by William Buckland, a local benefactor. The 'City of Refuge' relief on the wall is Royal Doulton. The eye-catching wooden windmill behind the church was built only a short time ago by a local who now lives in it. Cross the road and take the signposted public footpath, passing one of the Wraysbury Lakes on the right. Continue along this path to the junction with a gravel track. Veer left onto it and continue ahead along Tithe Lane to Station Road. Turn right and shortly pass Wraysbury station on the right.

2. Continue along Coppermill Road and immediately after crossing the bridge over Colne Brook, turn right onto a public footpath, following a Colne Valley Park sign. Follow the path as it skirts Colne Brook and then the railway line. The Wraysbury Reservoir is out of sight to the left. Go over a stile and veer left to follow its perimeter fence.

3. At the signpost a little way along this path, turn right to walk across the field towards the motorway. Continue ahead, keeping near to the railway line and following a yellow public footpath sign.

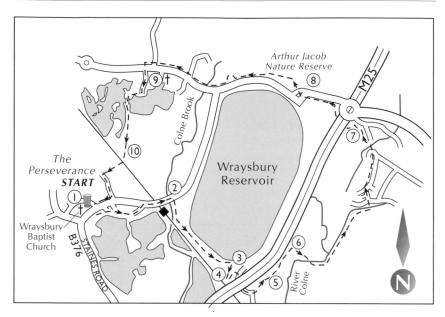

4. At a wire fence turn sharp left and then right over a stile into a paddock. Continue ahead. Go over a metal stile, turn right and follow the road as it veers left through the motorway underpass. Continue to the T-junction and turn left, following a sign for Stanwell Moor.

5. Immediately after crossing a bridge over a brook, turn right and go down the wooden steps and over a stile. Cross the field, go over another stile and veer left to cross a third stile. Go up the incline and turn left to follow the track of a former railway line.

6. At a crosspaths, turn right over a stile onto Staines Moor. Continue, first straight ahead and then veering slightly left to soon reach the River Colne. Facing the river, turn left and follow it to a footbridge. Cross this and continue in the same direction on the other side of the river. Cross another footbridge over a brook and continue to a kissing gate. Go through it and turn left onto a cement track, following a Colne Valley Way sign.

Continue ahead, cross a concrete bridge and turn left onto Hithermoor Road. Continue ahead to the T-junction and turn left onto Leylands Lane. When this road veers sharply left, go straight ahead to cross a footbridge over the river, to the left of a weir. Turn right, cross another footbridge and follow the path ahead. At the T-junction with another path, turn right, cross another bridge and continue ahead along a cement road.

7. At the T-junction cross straight over, turn left onto a bridleway signposted Poyle. Continue ahead as it turns left and goes through an underpass, along an M25 flyover and then through another underpass. Continue to Horton Road and turn left. Cross the bridge and continue to the roundabout.

8. Cross over to the right side of Horton Road, then cross Poyle Road and turn right onto it to walk past the Golden Cross pub. Turn left across the pub car park. Go through the wooden gate to enter Poyle Poplars Community Woodland Arthur Jacob Nature Reserve. Veer slightly right and continue along the path. Fork left at the wooden footbridge on the right, then turn right to follow the path as it runs close to the road. Keep on the path when it eventually veers right. At the fork keep left to walk across the car park. Turn left to leave the park and then right onto Stanwell Road. Pass the end of Coppermill Road on the left and then continue ahead to Horton village, passing Horton church on the left, before reaching the green on the right.

9. Just past the green, turn left onto Park Lane and continue ahead. When the road becomes a track, follow it as it curves right. Pass the kennels on the right, where you'll probably be barked at, but have no fear, there's a high fence between you and all the residents. Go over the footbridge then follow the footpath as it turns left. Continue ahead between two of the tree-fringed Wraysbury Lakes. Go over a footbridge and continue ahead to a T-junction with a gravel track.

10. Cross over here and continue ahead along a narrow grassy path, running to the left of the gravel path, and follow it as it veers left and goes over a footbridge. Continue ahead and cross a stile to the railway line. Cross the line with care, cross another stile and continue ahead to Douglas Lane. Walk along here and turn right onto Station Road. Continue ahead to reach the Perseverance pub on the right.

PLACES OF INTEREST NEARBY
Wraysbury village is well worth exploring further or you may wish to visit *Windsor* which is just six miles away. Apart from the obvious attraction of the castle and the historic town centre, there are several small museums. Telephone the Windsor Tourist Information Office on 01753 852010 for further details.

THE COLNE VALLEY WAY NEAR HARMONDSWORTH

This walk starts and finishes in an exciting new country park alongside the River Colne, Wraysbury River and Duke of Northumberland's River, as well as some artificial lakes, all of which attract water birds. The Colne Valley Way along Colne Brook closes the circle.

One of the lakes on Harmondsworth Moor

Just outside Harmondsworth is a cluster of minor rivers and a set of new artificial lakes, some not yet on maps. By its new headquarters, British Airways is currently rehabilitating wasteland to form a country park, Harmondsworth Moor. The public open space already created is wonderful for wildlife and ramblers. The walk starts by a large lake next to the HQ itself, and ends in the park alongside the River Colne. Amidst the attractively overgrown river banks are swans and herons; small islands also provide refuges for waterfowl. A large new lake nearby with reed beds is also a wildlife haven.

The middle section of the walk follows the Colne Valley Way along Colne Brook, a very pretty green corridor close to the M4 and M25. These roads and Heathrow Airport have isolated Harmondsworth itself from through traffic, making the surrounds a great place to walk. You may find that new sections of the park have opened around Pulpit Bridge, making it possible to bypass some of Accommodation Lane in point 2.

The Crown is a very friendly pub by the green in Harmondsworth, open all day and offering Bass and Courage Best real ales, together with a changing guest ale. Proper home-cooked food is a strong point here; lunch is served every day from 12 noon to 2.30 pm and evening meals from 6 pm to 9 pm. A full range from snacks to main meals is available – pay attention to the specials. You can enjoy your food in the bar, the separate dining area, or in the garden. Telephone: 020 8759 1007.

- **HOW TO GET THERE:** Harmondsworth is on the A3044, Holloway Lane/Hatch Lane between junction 4 on the M4 and the A4. Rail: West Drayton station is near point 8 and Iver near point 7. Buses: Route 81 (Hounslow to Slough) uses Bath Road at point 3.
- **PARKING:** At the car park in Accommodation Lane (point 2).
- **LENGTH OF THE WALK:** 7 miles. Map: OS Explorer 160 (GR 058778).

THE WALK

1. Leave the pub and turn left onto Moor Lane to pass the green and the end of Moorland Road. Cross the pretty humpback bridge over the Duke of Northumberland's River and turn left into Harmondsworth Moor country park, signposted 'Bath Road 670m'. Walk towards the new BA offices then, at the lake, turn right, signposted 'South Bridge 700m'. Turn right to leave the park by the kissing gate, signposted 'Pulpit Bridge 250m'. Come out opposite the car park and toilets.

2. Turn left onto Accommodation Lane and follow it down and round to the right past the entrance to the BA offices. The footpath ends here so cross over to the right. Just over the River Colne bridge the road turns left 90 degrees, but stay on the public footpath straight on through a kissing gate, along the Wraysbury River. Stay on the path as it turns left at a landscaped earthwork. Walk away from the river along the gravel path between the trees, meeting rabbits and low-flying aircraft. Just before the A4, do not walk up to the main road but follow the bridleway to the right, under the A4 by the river, passing the end of the old A4 bridge. Turn left and then right onto a continuation of the

39

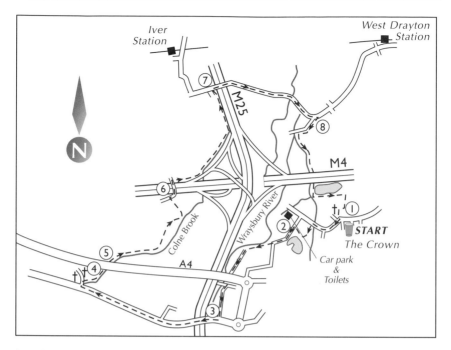

bridleway, an unmade track. Keep straight on, on the left of a field, following electric cables on wooden poles. Come out on Bath Road and turn right.

3. Cross the Wraysbury River and M25 (into Berkshire). Shortly after the disused railway, on the left is a preserved white pump, originally from Bath, re-erected here in 1827 as one of a number of pumps along the Colnbrook Turnpike. Walk through Poyle along Bath Road, lined by some large mature trees. The road, now Park Street, then enters Colnbrook, a characterful old village. Pass on the left the picturesque King John's Palace and the Star and Garter pub, then a London City marker at Colnbrook Bridge. Cross this – the road becomes Bridge Street.

4. Turn right into Mill Street at the 15th/16th century Ye Old George pub. Veer left beside Colne Brook. Behind the stream is a striking white building, presumably once the mill. Note the large old barn behind. Continue up the road and then straight along the path at the end, ignoring a footpath sign to the left. Follow the Colne Valley Way signpost and keep right of the transport café and car park. Cross the

A4 beside the bridge and enter the double gateway there (this is also a bridleway).

5. Keep by Colne Brook on the right. When the bridleway and path separate, the footpath stays by the river, marked by yellow arrows on tree trunks. The bridleway is easier to follow, marked by blue arrows on stakes. Over on the right is a large body of water. Cross a stile where footpath and bridleway meet – the path is now fenced on both sides. Go through a gate and turn right. The path and bridleway may be confused here. On the left is a pond and on the right a large reed-fringed lake, a magnet for waterfowl.

6. Take the bridge over the M4. At field level again, turn right at the traffic barrier (Colne Valley Way signpost by power cables), walk back to the M4 along the right edge of the field, then turn left following the signs. Leave the field in the corner by the motorway through wooden baffles and follow the well-defined wooded path by the side of the next field but separated from it by a hedge. At Colne Brook turn left and follow the path round. This is a beautiful green corridor here, right by the motorway. Just by the bridge over the brook is a Colne Valley Way information board: do not go through the kissing gate or under the bridge, but keep left, with the fence on your right, and the open field on your left. At the end of the footpath leave to the right (past a 'Restored Quarry' sign) through the wooden baffles. Go up the steps and turn right.

7. Cross the road (Thorney Mill Road) and follow it over the M25. Ignore any further Colne Valley Way signs – keep straight on past the golf course on the left and the picnic site on the right. Cross a watercourse, the disused railway and a stream to enter the London Borough of Hillingdon. On the left pass the entrance to the nature reserve. Cross the River Colne; on the left is a former watermill, now redeveloped, but the old mill wheel is still there in the millrace. Cross Frays River, which meets the Colne here, then turn right into Cricketfield Road.

8. Continue past the cricket club and caravan site entrance. Just before the bridge turn left through the metal kissing gate onto the path following the river through the meadow, first grass, then gravel. Go through a wooden kissing gate and take the right-hand gravel path through a landscaped meadow to the left of the pond. Cross the pond by the footbridge and head towards the M4 bridge. Go under the M4 and follow the path. Take the right fork at the large rectangular reed-edged lake. The river veers away from the path – just downstream the Duke of Northumberland's River comes off the River Colne. At a junction take the left fork signposted 'Harmondsworth' and walk round the lake. At its end, go through a kissing gate onto a footpath and turn right. Continue through a metal gate into the churchyard; take the path leading diagonally towards the main path by the church. Just to the right of this junction, under the tree, is the large flat tomb of Richard Cox (of apple fame) and his wife Ann. Exit the churchyard by the main gate and come to the village green. Turn left to return to the Crown.

PLACES OF INTEREST NEARBY

Frays Island Nature Reserve is on an island formed where Frays River meets the Colne, near the watermill just outside West Drayton. It is run by the London Wildlife Trust.

IVER: TWO CANALS, TWO RIVERS AND A LAKE

Starting from Packet Boat Lane, Cowley Peachey, you walk briefly along the towpaths of rural stretches of the Grand Union Canal and the Slough Arm, before reaching pleasant Iver village, from where you take a delightful woodland path between two bodies of water, the River Colne and Little Britain Lake. You then stroll along tranquil Old Mill Lane by Frays River, before returning to the pub along another stretch of the Grand Union Canal towpath.

The Grand Union Canal at Cowley Peachey

Packet Boat Lane derives its name from the Paddington Packet Boat which in 1801 began taking passengers from here along the canal to Paddington. The horse-drawn boat took almost a day to complete its journey.

The Slough Arm is a long, straight, lock-free branch of five miles that ends near Slough station. The first part is rural and rich in wildlife,

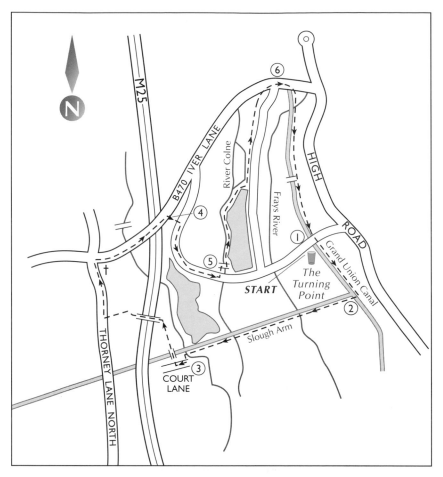

with three aqueducts that take the canal over Colne Brook and the Colne and Frays rivers. Both Colne Brook and Frays River were important for powering mills. The latter was constructed by a Mr Frays, a local landowner, to serve six mills in the area, one of which is seen on the walk.

The walk begins at the Turning Point pub, beautifully positioned right next to the canal. Its name refers to the winding or turning point in the pub's backyard where the widening in the canal enables 60 foot narrow boats to turn. The tables and chairs out here are a glorious suntrap in summer and you can watch canal life going by as you enjoy a leisurely drink or meal. There is an extensive bar menu, for outside or in the comfortable bars, and a separate restaurant offers specialities such as poached skate wing or beef stroganoff. Food is served Monday to Saturday from 12.30 pm to 9.30 pm and Sunday 12 noon to 4 pm. Beers served include Bass and London Pride. Children may be brought into the restaurant, but not in the main bar. Telephone: 01895 440550.

- **HOW TO GET THERE:** The pub is at Canal Cottages in Packet Boat Lane, just west of the canal bridge; turn left off the A408 (heading north) in Cowley Peachey. Rail: West Drayton station then walk northwards along the towpath to the pub. Underground: Uxbridge (Metroplitan and, peak only, Piccadilly Lines) then bus 222 or take the towpath to join the walk at Iver Lane.
- **PARKING:** The pub car park can get busy – use roadside parking along Packet Boat Lane or in the industrial area on the other side of the bridge.
- **LENGTH OF THE WALK:** 4 miles. Map: OS Explorer 172 (GR 054812).

THE WALK

1. From the pub, cross the canal and turn right onto the towpath. Continue the short distance to Cowley Peachey Junction where the Slough Arm begins.

2. Go over the footbridge across the Grand Union Canal here, to reach the Slough Arm towpath. Continue ahead, passing over the Frays River, the River Colne and Colne Brook.

3. Just after the third aqueduct, turn left to leave the canal. Turn right onto Court Lane, and right again to cross the footbridge over the canal. Continue ahead along a grassy path running to the left of the approach road to the Thames Water Utilities sewage works. Cross the M25 by the footbridge, and continue along a path to the left of a wooden fence, and then on a cement track to the right of a field. At the T-junction with Thorney Lane North turn right and continue ahead to Iver. At St Peter's church turn right onto Iver Lane and continue ahead to cross the bridge over the M25.

4. Immediately after this bridge turn right and descend the cement steps to Ford Lane. Turn right and walk along the pavement on the left, and when this ends continue along the grass verge. Keep going when the road becomes a wide dirt track.

5. When the track veers sharp right, veer left onto a path signposted 'Colne Valley Way'. Turn right to cross the bridge over the River Colne, and then turn left through the kissing gate and continue ahead. You are now walking between two bodies of water, the River Colne and Little Britain Lake. Take time to appreciate this section of the walk. There is always something special about walking with water on each side of you, and this is a peaceful, shady path. The river and the lake are usually lined by anglers. The trees and all this water make it a good spot for birdwatching. The Colne path ends just before a weir on the left and at the end of the lake on the right. Turn right at the small picnic area. Walk across the grass and turn left at Old Mill Lane. Walk along the grassy bank of Frays River, as there is no footpath. Continue on the left as the verge ends.

Now you see where the lane gets its name – the derelict old mill house on the right, with Frays River as a mill race. An old mill by the stream, but if you start singing *Nellie Dean*, you spent too long in the pub.

6. At the end of the lane turn right onto Iver Lane, cross the Cowley Bridge over the canal and turn right to join the towpath just before the lock. Go past Cowley Lock and the keeper's cottage. Boat users are grateful for the fact that you can travel from here and then on the Paddington Arm and Regent's Canal without encountering another lock until Camden. Follow the towpath along the recreation area, under a low bridge, past more moorings and then leave it at the next humpback bridge to return to the pub.

PLACES OF INTEREST NEARBY

Langley Country Park and the adjoining *Black Park Country Park* straddle the A412, four miles north-west of Cowley Peachey; they consist of farmland, mixed woodland, formal gardens and picnic areas with signposted footpaths winding through the most attractive areas.

There is a car park in Langley Country Park on the west side of Billet Lane, and the southern entrance to Langley Country Park is a ten minute walk from Langley station which is one stop from Iver station. Information is available at the Centenary Lodge Visitor Centre, Black Park Country Park, Black Park Road, Wexham. Telephone: 01753 511060.

THE GRAND UNION CANAL, PADDINGTON ARM AND RIVER BRENT

❧❦❧

This varied route starts by the Grand Union Canal and continues to Greenford along the towpath which is surprisingly rural, flanked by reeds and wildflowers. After walking through Ravenor Park a path by the Brent is taken to Brent Lodge Park in Hanwell where there is a small zoo. From here you follow the river under the Wharncliffe Viaduct, and then through woodland back to the Grand Union Canal towpath.

The entrance to the Willow Tree Marina

The Paddington Arm of the Grand Union Canal extends 13 miles from Bull's Bridge to Paddington. It was opened in 1801. There are no tunnels or locks, so it offers a swift passage for long boats.

The walk begins at the Grand Junction Arms pub which overlooks the canal just west of the Western Road bridge. It's a congenial place

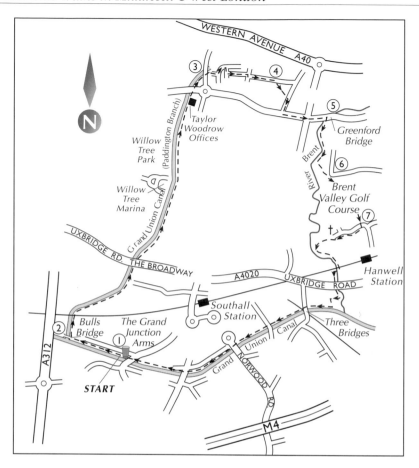

with a huge, friendly beige cat and an extensive menu of bar snacks and dishes such as beef and ale pie. The draught beer is John Smith's Smooth and the lagers include Holsten, Foster's and Kronenbourg. Food is served seven days a week from 12 noon till 9.30 pm. Children are allowed in the pub and garden at all times if they are eating, otherwise until 7 pm. Telephone: 020 8813 9242.

- **HOW TO GET THERE:** The starting point is on Bulls Bridge Road, just beyond the Western Road bridge over the canal. Take the A312 and then Hayes Road which becomes Western Road at the canal bridge. Rail: Southall and Hanwell stations are both near the walk. Buses: you can also join the walk by taking route 95 to Ruislip Road or route 207 to Uxbridge Road.

- **PARKING:** In the pub car park but please seek permission before leaving your car whilst you walk. Also there is a car park opposite Hanwell church (point 7).
- **LENGTH OF THE WALK:** 10 miles. Map: OS Explorer 173 (GR 114788).

THE WALK

1. From the pub turn right onto the towpath and proceed ahead.

2. Just before Bull's Bridge, veer right and then turn right onto the Paddington Arm towpath, following a Hillingdon Trail sign. Continue ahead, to go under a railway bridge and eventually the Uxbridge Road bridge. Once under the bridge, continue ahead, passing a housing estate on the right and modern town houses on the left, after which the canal becomes rural again. Continue ahead under a footbridge, just after which is the Willow Tree Marina on the left. Continue under an elegant arched footbridge, built in 1982. Just past the bridge is the attractive Willow Tree Park on the left. Go under the Taylor-Woodrow offices which span the canal and then under the Ruislip Road and Kensington Road bridges.

3. Immediately after the Kensington Road bridge, turn right, ascend the steps and turn left onto a footpath. Continue ahead, and at Marley Close turn left and then left again onto Ferrymead Avenue, and then right onto Rosedene Avenue. Turn left onto Crossmead Avenue and continue ahead. At the T-junction turn right and then left onto Ravenor Park Road, and continue ahead.

4. Turn right onto a wide tarmac track between houses and continue ahead into Ravenor Park. Local landlord George Ravenor owned Ravenor Farm in the late 19th century, and the park stands on his former farmland. At the first crosstracks turn left and proceed ahead. After passing a children's playground on the right leave the park and turn right onto Oldfield Lane. Continue ahead and turn left at the T-junction onto The Broadway. Cross over at the lights and continue in the same direction crossing Greenford Road and Greenford Bridge.

5. Immediately after the bridge, turn right and descend the steps to the river path, part of Brent River Park managed to conserve wildlife and provide interesting walks. Continue along the left bank. Stay on the path as it veers left and away from the river, keeping near the wooden fence on the right.

6. At the T-junction turn left, and then immediately right and continue ahead. At the fork turn left to walk away from the river. At the next T-junction, just before a children's playground on the left, turn right. Continue along this track which cuts through Brent Valley Golf Course, ignoring all turn offs to the left.

7. At Church Road turn right and continue ahead along the pavement on the left and then on the tarmac track that skirts Churchfields Recreation Ground. Pass a car park on the left and, facing Hanwell church, turn left into Brent Lodge Park. Continue ahead on the main path to reach the zoo.

Pass the Animal Centre and a café on the left and keep on this track as it veers left to follow the left bank of the Brent. Go through a metal kissing gate and continue ahead. At the fork bear right, and then turn right through a wooden kissing gate. Go under the viaduct bridge. At the T-junction turn right to cross the river and then go left to walk along the right bank.

Cross busy Uxbridge Road with care. Continue straight ahead along the delightful woodland path called Fitzherbert Walk, which is also part of Brent River Park. Near the water's edge there is a good mix of shrubs and wildflowers.

8. Soon after passing a couple of picnic benches on the right, veer right and ascend the steps to the Grand Union Canal towpath. Turn right and continue ahead passing the Hanwell flight of locks – there are six locks in all. Behind the brick wall on the right are the buildings of Ealing Hospital. Continue ahead to the Windmill Lane bridge where there is a unique road, rail and canal crossing known as Three Bridges; built to Brunel's design in 1855. Continue ahead, going under several bridges. Go under the bridge at Western Road to return to the Grand Junction Arms.

PLACES OF INTEREST NEARBY

The small zoo in *Brent Lodge Park* (usually open during daylight hours) is a delight for children. The fascinating outdoor enclosures are free and the indoor Animal Centre (admission charge) houses a variety of small mammals and reptiles. Telephone: 020 8758 5916.

ISLEWORTH TO OSTERLEY: A CANAL AND RIVER CIRCUIT

The walk starts at a beautiful spot on the Thames, then passes through Syon Park to follow artificial waterways and visit Osterley House to admire the efforts of landscape gardeners. Luckily the wildlife along the route thrives, despite the fact that the habitat is not natural.

Osterley Lock

The Grand Union Canal was a triumph of engineering of the 18th century to provide a major transport route to and from the Port of London. The section used for this walk was built to improve navigation along the Brent. The basins at Brentford near the union of the canal and the Brent with the Thames are reminders of the canal's industrial life. The Duke of Northumberland's River was dug in the 16th century to carry water from the Colne valley to watermills in Isleworth, near the Duke's house at Syon. The mills are gone, although you will walk down a lane called Mill Plat, the canal mainly carries leisure craft, and

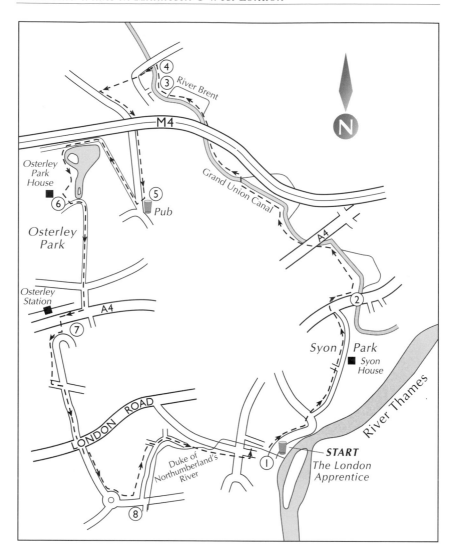

the artificial waterways have become green corridors – much of the outward route is through the Brent River Park.

These two waterways are used in this walk to connect two of London's finest stately homes, Syon House and Osterley House. Both feature much work by Robert Adam and are architectural gems. The grounds of Osterley House, owned by the National Trust, may be roamed freely, and the walk passes through them by the lakes.

The London Apprentice is a riverside pub in a lovely position on

Church Street by Isleworth Ait. It has been welcoming visitors since 1760, when apprentices came by river on their day off. The views are great, particularly of the birds at low tide. The pub is open all day seven days a week, serving Marston's Pedigree, Old Speckled Hen and Courage Directors and Best ales. The choice of food is wide at lunchtimes and evenings (not Sunday evening, but you can eat between 12 noon and 5 pm) and the Tavern menu offers hot food cooked to order, daily specials and Sunday roasts, plus desserts, in the bar and dining area; you can even have tea made at the bar. A gourmet menu is available in the separate Riverside Restaurant. Telephone: 020 8560 1915.

- **HOW TO GET THERE:** Turn off the A315, London Road, just west of Syon Park onto Twickenham Road (A310) then almost immediately after onto Park Road, which becomes Church Street by the river. The route passes Osterley station (Piccadilly Line) at point 7.
- **PARKING:** In Syon Park or Osterley Park (fee – the latter is free to NT members).
- **LENGTH OF THE WALK:** 8 miles. Map: OS Explorer 161 (GR 167760).

THE WALK

1. Leave the pub and walk by the river past the manor house, with its blue plaque to Arthur Penty, and Swan House with its balcony next door. Continue past All Saints' church, rebuilt after being burnt down in the Second World War (by schoolboys, not the Luftwaffe). Follow the road round to the left away from the Thames and turn right through the gates into Syon Park. Walk through the park, which gives the illusion of countryside, passing the house and associated buildings to the main London Road. Cross at the pelican crossing and turn right.

2. Just before the canal bridge turn left onto the towpath and walk along the canal, passing Brentford Gauging Lock. Go through a kissing gate and over a footbridge past the large basin and a signpost to Braunston: '93 miles'. The towpath is overhung by old industrial sheds, where we found graffiti quoting T.S. Eliot. Back on the open towpath, go under a bridge, then the main A4 road bridge. Walk past a wooden footbridge and through the metal kissing gate to come to Clitheroe's Lock. Cross the canal at the next footbridge and go under the Piccadilly Line viaduct. Go past the entrance to Brent River Park under the M4 bridge and over the footbridge crossing the arm of the Brent. Continue on to Osterley Lock. To the right is an arm of the River Brent. On the lockside area note the patterned bricks underfoot, made at Elthorne Park High School in 1999 with themes reflecting this green corridor.

3. Continue past Osterley Lock over the footbridge – do not miss the beautiful view to the right of the arm of the Brent. The river and canal are combined as you continue along this green route – you may see herons. Pass a sign: 'British Waterways; Kerr Cup Pile Driving Competition; prize length of piling 1959'. Behind this is an overgrown orchard – but don't go scrumping through the nearby hole in the fence.

4. Just before a metal bridge over the canal, turn right up steep curving steps and turn left to cross the canal, leaving Brent River Park through a kissing gate. Cross the railway line with care. At the other side, follow the path away from the railway alongside the sports ground. Go through a kissing gate to the main road and turn left. Approach the M4 bridge. On your left is Long Wood – a mixed broad-leaf wood that is a good birdwatching site. Go under the M4 and past the Hare and Hounds.

5. Just past the pub (a couple of yards only!) cross over and go through (not across) the railings to take an overgrown path that comes out at the left of the two gatehouses. Turn right and follow the track between them. Follow the track between the lakes (note the view of Osterley House to the left) and round to the left at the end, then enter the tall kissing gate in the fence on the left. Walk to the right by the lake. Exit from the trees near an island in the lake and head off across the grass to the half-right. Keep the lake on the left, going past the fine trees at its edge, and continue on to turn left through the gate. You could visit the house now if open.

6. Otherwise pass the Chinese-style pavilion (which rotates) in the lake. Follow the tree-lined drive away from the house to the main exit and go straight down Thornbury Road. Turn right at the Great West Road, walk along to the tube station and go down into the subway.

7. Leave the subway by the right-hand exit. Follow the path, turning left at the end, along the Piccadilly Line. At the footbridge, cross the line, then turn left. Come to a road (Spring Grove), turn left under the railway bridge, then turn right into Worton Way. Continue at the end down the passageway, crossing the main road, and go straight down Bridge Road. At the roundabout fork left down Worton Road.

8. Turn left at Riverside Walk along the Duke of Northumberland's River, a welcome bit of urban greenery. Follow it round to the right down a track, ignore the footbridge and follow the path as it becomes an alleyway. Come out opposite St John's Centre near Coppermill Drive. Turn right, following the signposted Riverside Walk to Old Isleworth. Opposite the start of St John's Gardens turn right, cross the bridge over the river and turn left, following the path to Shire Horse Way – this used to be a brewery. Turn left and then right at the roundabout to follow the river and continue along the road as the river disappears underground. At the end of St John's Road turn left into Twickenham Road, cross over, pass the end of Sarah Sermon's Almshouses (1849) and the end of North Street, then turn right into Silverhall Neighbourhood Park. Follow the river through the fine trees. Turn left at the fence at the end to go over the bridge, then turn right down the narrow path. Pass the Ingram Almshouses of 1664. Pass the former entrance to Warkworth on the left. The Duke of Northumberland's River ends at Kidds Mill Sluice – the waters flow into a pool and then into the Thames. Old Isleworth is to the right. Turn left; follow the Thames Path to the left along Church Street, passing several fine buildings to return to the pub.

PLACES OF INTEREST NEARBY

Syon House, the seat of the Dukes of Northumberland, is open spring to autumn, Wednesday, Thursday, Sunday and public holidays; the gardens are open all year except at Christmas. Admission fee. Telephone: 020 8560 0883.

Osterley House is a showcase of architect Robert Adam's work. Open from April to the end of October, Wednesday to Sunday (not Good Friday) plus Bank Holiday Mondays. Admission fee; free to NT members. Telephone: 020 8758 3918.

PUTNEY TO MORTLAKE:
THE BOAT RACE

This linear walk by the Thames from Putney Bridge to Chiswick Bridge leads you along the Middlesex side of the route of the Oxford and Cambridge Boat Race – past exceptional riverside and some of London's swankiest addresses.

The Thames near Chiswick

The course of the University Boat Race must be the most famous section of the Thames, being seen by millions each year on television. Most viewers will not concentrate on the scenery, which is a pity, as this is one of the most beautiful sections of the river, especially at low tide, when water birds flock to the mud banks to feed. If you can combine low tide with early evening, it is a magical sight.

As befits anything to do with rowers, there are numerous pubs along this part of the river. Close to the start of the race, on the Putney side at 8 Lower Richmond Road, the Duke's Head is well thought of.

Telephone: 020 8788 2552. Around the middle, just after Hammersmith Bridge, are many good pubs, most offering a view of the river. At the Mortlake end Ye White Hart, on The Terrace in Barnes, has open terraces overlooking the river. It has a large wooden-floored bar inside, and takes great pride in its wine range. A Young's house, it also has Young's Special and Bitter ales. Food is served at lunchtimes seven days a week, with roasts on Sundays. Telephone: 020 8876 5177.

- **HOW TO GET THERE:** Putney Bridge is on the A219 in Fulham. Underground: Putney Bridge (District Line). This is not a circular walk; the end is near National Rail stations Barnes Bridge and Mortlake, and Underground Kew Gardens (District Line).
- **PARKING:** Best by public transport. Alternatively, you could park near the end at Dukes Meadows (in point 6), cross the river on Barnes Bridge, and walk across Barnes Common down Lower Richmond Road to Putney Bridge.
- **LENGTH OF THE WALK:** 5 miles. Map: OS Explorer 161 (GR 243759).

THE WALK

1. Start by the river in Bishop's Park next to Putney Bridge. On the opposite bank are a number of boathouses and a marker for the start line of the Boat Race. You are on the side usually taken by the crew that loses the toss, because of the long pull round the bend at Hammersmith. The race is not run against the flow, but is timed to take advantage of an incoming tide. Walk alongside the river or through Bishops Park on your right, which has a café, toilets, a paddling pool and a wildfowl pool, home to moorhens, mallard, pochard and tufted duck. At the end of the waterfront, turn right to detour along Stevenage Road around Fulham Football Ground, Craven Cottage.

2. Immediately after the end of the ground, turn left to resume the Thames Path. Turn right at the river and continue towards Hammersmith Bridge, opposite open land that is being developed into a wildlife reserve. This part of the river is rich in birdlife; at low tide herons, cormorants and gulls make a spectacle for birdwatchers. Many former wharves have been redeveloped for housing, providing a new river path. However, Palace Wharf is still inaccessible. So follow the detour passing the Crabtree Tavern, turning right then immediately left down a walkway to turn left onto Rainville Road. Turn left again down an alleyway back to the riverfront and continue towards Hammersmith.

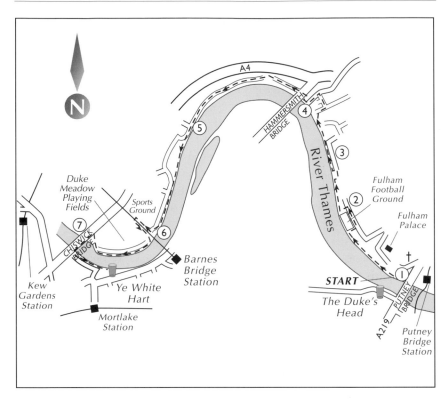

3. Just after, on the right, is architect Richard Rogers's headquarters, with a display window featuring models of the partnership's designs. The large building with twin towers on the other side of the river is Harrods' Depository, a Boat Race landmark. At the time of writing, a short detour around a fenced-off redevelopment is necessary, before leaving the river to walk round the Riverside Studios theatre along Crisp Road. Turn left at the end to walk back to the river along Queen Caroline Street.

4. Walk under Hammersmith Bridge and pass the Blue Anchor and Rutland Ale House pubs. Walk through Furnivale Gardens and at the end turn right, then first left into an alleyway, passing the Dove. Pass the sailing club lookout and walk through the archway ahead. Pass the Old Ship pub and go through more gardens. At the end turn right, then left at the pub to walk down Hammersmith Terrace. These mansions have gardens extending right up to the river. Many still have roman numerals on the front doors; the author A.P. Herbert lived at number XII. Pass Lovat, a useful corner shop at Eyot Gardens and Chiswick Mall. Continue down

Chiswick Mall; this cuts off the impressive houses on the right from their private gardens and moorings on the left. Inch-thick glass plates instead of front railings are flood precautions. The island on the left is Chiswick Eyot. Birdlife makes this area especially appealing at low tide. Just past the end of the island the path comes down to the river; further along, gardens again intervene. Arrive at a bend in the road. Chiswick church is ahead on the right; the tomb of the artist Hogarth, surrounded by railings, is on the river side.

5. Just before the church, at the end of Chiswick Mall, is a slipway down to the water. Pass this and turn left straight after it onto a private gated pathway, open to pedestrians during daylight hours, then turn right onto the new riverside walkway. Pass a brasserie, then continue along Thames Crescent – this is private, but access is granted to pedestrians. Take a tarmac path through grassland, which continues as a dirt path by the river. Come to open grassland with stone terracing on the right, a view of Barnes on the left and Barnes railway bridge ahead. Turn right at the end of the grassland, following a Thames Path signpost, and come to the railway.

6. For a short cut to Barnes Bridge station, turn left and cross the footbridge. Otherwise, turn right at the railway line and, opposite Riverside Health Club, turn left under the railway bridge, then left again. Pass Dukes Hollow nature reserve and follow the road past Chiswick Boat House and a small car park. Then, as the road veers to the right, either take a small possibly overgrown riverside path or follow the road. Just before the next boathouse, Tideway Scullers School, you can see a blue and white post near the river bank – this is the finishing post for the Boat Race. Go on to Chiswick Bridge.

7. Go up the steps. At the end of the race, the boats coast on under the bridge, and the exhausted crews step out at the boathouse beyond. The walk finishes here also. Cross the river, and either turn right to head for Kew Gardens station, or go down the steps on the left and walk back along Thames Bank, to reach Ye White Hart or the railway stations.

PLACES OF INTEREST NEARBY
Fulham Palace by Putney Bridge is open in the afternoons on Wednesday to Sunday plus Bank Holiday Mondays; admission fee. Telephone: 020 7736 3233.

THE GRAND UNION CANAL AND RIVER BRENT AT GREENFORD

Two waterways make for a long green walk in an area more known for industry, but which hosts a variety of wildlife and one of London's beauty spots.

The canal at Perivale

The Paddington Arm of the Grand Union Canal may have originally been built for industrial reasons, but it has been there for over 200 years, now providing a valuable green corridor to connect open countryside to isolated beauty spots like Horsenden Hill. The fact that it is artificial, however, provides you with one unique experience – seeing a boat glide peacefully along the aqueduct over the North Circular Road. The Brent River Park offers a contrasting natural route through a very developed area.

    The canal is home to a surprising amount of wildlife – birds you can see include swallows, herons and kingfishers. In Alperton there is great competition for the fish in the canal – we witnessed crows chasing off herons who perch on the bank looking for small pike, and heard fishermen's tales of better fishing, and larger carp, further on…

You can eat more comfortably at the Black Horse, a justifiably popular pub right on the canal in Oldfield Lane North, Greenford. It is by a turning point and watering point on the canal and has recently been redeveloped to make more of its canalside position. Excellent meals are served seven days a week, and this Fuller's house naturally serves these well-loved London ales. Arrive early for weekday lunches, as the place is well patronised by staff from nearby offices. Telephone: 020 8578 1384.

- **HOW TO GET THERE:** Oldfield Lane North can be reached from the A4127, Greenford Road. Rail: Greenford station (Central Line and National Rail) is near to the pub. The walk passes close to Alperton (Piccadilly Line) and Hanger Lane (Central Line), both of which have toilets.
- **PARKING:** Ask before using the pub car park – you'll be gone a long time and the pub is popular. You may find street parking around Perivale, and there is a car park for Pitshanger Park off Bellevue Road.
- **LENGTH OF THE WALK:** 10 miles (5¼ miles if taking short cut at point 6). Map: OS Explorer 173 (GR 149845).

THE WALK

1. Take the path down to the towpath and walk away from the bridge past the pub gardens with the canal on your right. Go through the kissing gate, under a pipe bridge and road bridge. The towpath crosses a bridge over the entrance to a basin.

2. Pass possibly the largest mosque in Europe. Go under the footbridge, through a kissing gate and under the A40 bridge. The open, wild surrounds, a former farm and orchards, are now Smith's Farm, part of Northolt and Greenford Countryside Park. Go about 30 yards past another footbridge and turn left onto the first good gravel path, then right at a crossroads. Turn left where the path rejoins the towpath, past hawthorn trees.

3. Just before the next road bridge turn left onto the path up and away from the canal. Walk along Kensington Road away from the canal. Just

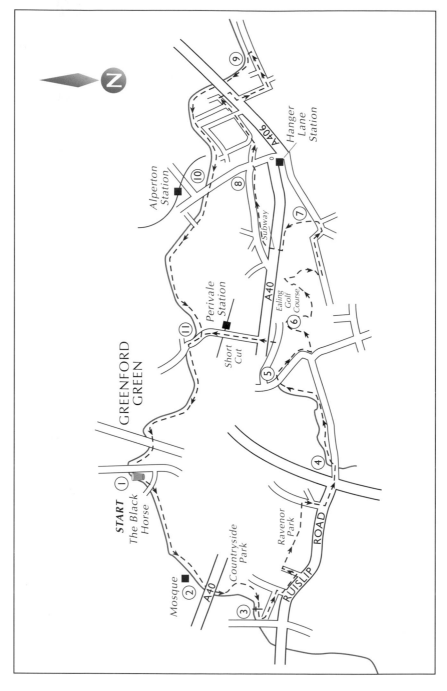

past St Hugh's church, turn left through the break in the bushes into the end of Gosling Close, then turn right at the end into Ferrymead Avenue. Turn left at the main Ruislip Road and then left into Eastmead Avenue. Pass the end of Stickleton Close and turn right into Ravenor Park, a quiet refuge with some fine trees. At a T-junction head half-right across the grass. Join a tarmac path near the end of the tennis courts; pass the end of an avenue of poplars, following a line of oaks. Go to the right of the children's play area and leave the park, turning right onto Oldfield Lane. Pass the library, turn left onto Ruislip Road, and keep straight across the main Greenford Road.

4. Cross the River Brent at Greenford Bridge, then immediately afterwards turn left onto the Brent River Park Walk. The path now leads through a narrow but very wild strip of land on the right of the Brent. Follow this past a weir and an inlet into the river. There is a golf course on the opposite side, but the right bank is still good wildlife habitat despite its proximity to the road. Take to the pavement briefly, then resume the river bank path just before the railway bridge. Follow the Brent past a swimming pool on your right.

5. Just after the river passes under the Argyle Road bridge, turn left onto the pavement, then turn right, following Brent River Park Walk signs. Cross the road with care and walk to the traffic lights. Do not continue down the road, but turn left onto a footpath (signposted to Perivale Lane) going down the left of playing fields, then allotments; shrubs and brambles hide the river on your left. Keep straight on over a crossing path to walk between fences. The path goes through a short wooded area, then a golf course, shielded by hedges.

6. Join a path just before a bridge over the Brent. You can take a short cut here by turning left, crossing the Brent, continuing on to the A40, crossing the footbridge, turning off the A40 into Horsenden Lane South, and following this past Perivale station to turn left onto the canal towpath and resume the walk at point 11. Otherwise turn right onto the other fenced path across this scenic golf course. At the end, turn left into Pitshanger Park. Walk to the tennis courts; the river is on your left, behind chestnut trees. At the next fork, the signposted route forks right, to the park gates. Alternatively, follow the river, then walk back through the park to the main gates. Turn left onto Meadvale Road. At the end, turn right into Neville Road, left into Brunswick Road, and just before Brentham Way opposite, turn left into a signposted alleyway.

7. Cross the stile and walk straight across Brentham Meadows, part of Brent River Park. Wild grasses and bushes provide flowers and seeds for insects, small mammals and birds. Walk to the left of the fenced pond, following an obvious grass track to the road. Turn left, walk over the Brent bridge, then take the subway under the A40, coming up the steps into Alperton Lane. Continue under the Central Line bridge and past the park to the end.

8. Cross Hanger Lane, turn right and immediately left into Riverside Gardens, just before the bridge. The Brent here is channelled but still has some wild habitat on the bank. Go halfway round the turning circle at the end of the road and then follow the public footpath sign down the drive to walk beside the river. Go under the imposing brick Piccadilly Line viaduct. The path opens out into a small wooded green left of the river. Pass a weir. At the footbridge turn left then right to keep on the grass. Walk along a series of grassy mounds close by the river. At the end, follow the footpath, then gated road, by the river. Pass a footbridge and the end of Water Road; turn right at the T-junction. Walk to the North Circular Road and turn right out of Abbeydale Road. Go down the subway ramp, under the road, up the steps and head straight on, away from the North Circular Road along Iveagh Avenue. Walk along to a T-junction with Twyford Abbey Road. Turn left, then continue past industrial buildings until the road meets the canal.

9. Turn left onto the towpath and walk back by the canal. Even in this industrial area it is flanked by trees laced with ivy. Cross the aqueduct over the North Circular Road and enjoy the spectacular view. The Middlesex arms are displayed between the two channels. A few paces from the end of the bridge, down to the left through thick undergrowth you can see the Brent, just before a new metal fence. Go under the footbridge past the remains of a line of poplars. Keep on the towpath under another footbridge and straight on past more poplars. Go under the Piccadilly Line and past some fine willows on the right to the road bridge by a striking blue building close to Alperton station.

10. Pass some long-term narrowboat moorings. Go under the brick Manor Farm Road bridge. After the towpath becomes a gravel path, go through a metal kissing gate. Pass many moorings on the right and note

Horsenden Hill ahead. On the right, after the moorings, the view becomes more open and there is a golf course. Horsenden Hill appears through the trees.

11. Go under a brick bridge carrying Horsenden Lane (with a separate footbridge). On the left, after a small open space, is Perivale Wood, a fenced-off wildlife reserve. This stretch of the canal, with its overgrown right bank, is particularly rich in birdlife. As you approach a footbridge you pass open meadowland on the left, behind the trees. Stay on the towpath beyond the footbridge and go under the road bridge (Greenford Road) and the next bridge to return to the pub.

PLACES OF INTEREST NEARBY
The giant *Hindu Temple* in Brentfield Road, Neasden, is an amazing sight. The walk passes what is said to be the largest mosque in Europe; this is the first traditional Hindu temple in Europe. Open to visitors daily from 9 am to 6 pm. There is an introductory display, for which there is an admission fee; otherwise the temple is free. Telephone 020 8965 2651.

WALK 14

YEADING BROOK IN NORTH AND WEST HARROW

This linear walk is an easy stroll through pleasant parts of Metroland, in the flatter parts of Harrow, much of the time with only greenery in sight.

The brook near Ruislip Gardens

Yeading Brook in Harrow is really a minor river, flowing past the end of suburban gardens, through parks and the remnants of meadows. The walk follows this green strip that is a well-kept secret, except among locals, who walk their dogs along it or play in it, depending on age. Occasional parks with mown lawns and some exotic trees and shrubs alternate with the remnants of meadows, grass verges, the edges of recreation grounds and bits of wilderness, and for much of the route the brook meanders within natural banks, so there is a rich variety of habitat. In the middle of suburbia, you feel at times in the countryside. A reminder of the power of nature is the fact that Yeading Brook can flood rapidly – some of the path may not be accessible after very heavy rain.

An attractive feature of J. J. Moon's (19-20 The Broadwalk, Pinner Road) is the delicious home-cooked food, which includes an all-day breakfast, grilled salmon, steak chasseur, daily specials, vegetarian options and roasts on Sunday. Three to five cask ales are served, including Courage Best and Fuller's London Pride. Although not a pub for children, the service is friendly, you can get tea and coffee with a couple of free refills, and you can sit in comfortable booths decorated with angling prints. Telephone: 020 8424 9686.

- **HOW TO GET THERE:** This is not a circular walk and is best reached by public transport. The start is near North Harrow station (Metropolitan Line) and the walk ends at Ruislip Gardens (Central Line). Rayners Lane (Metropolitan and Piccadilly Lines) is very close to point 3. The pub is on the short section of Pinner Road where the A404 and A4090 coincide, just opposite Canterbury Road.
- **PARKING:** There is parking in Cambridge Road, between the pub and North Harrow station, and at Headstone Manor (see Places of Interest Nearby).
- **LENGTH OF THE WALK:** 3½ miles. Map: OS Explorer 173 (GR 133887).

THE WALK

1. Leave the pub, turn right and, at the roundabout, right again onto Station Road. Go under the railway bridge and turn right onto Northumberland Road. Take the second turning left – opposite Headstone Scout hut – onto Yeading Walk, a tarmac path beside the brook, edged with shrubs, wild habitat and numerous trees including bamboo and willow. Follow this path, keeping the stream on your right and ignoring two footbridges. Cross the road, Rayners Lane, still keeping the stream on your right, and follow the path down to some crazy paving leading onto a footbridge. Cross the stream and continue to Whittington Way. Streamside access finishes here, so cross over, turn left and go back to the roundabout, admiring streamside fir trees on the corner. You are in the heart of Harrow Garden Village, developed in the 1930s by the Metropolitan Railway. The planners made sure there were green spaces and trees.

2. Take the first right, Church Avenue. At the end, enter Streamside Open Space, which is fairly wild and has more birdlife near the stream. Follow a concrete path down to cross a footbridge and continue left, roughly following the stream, which is now wider. There is no path,

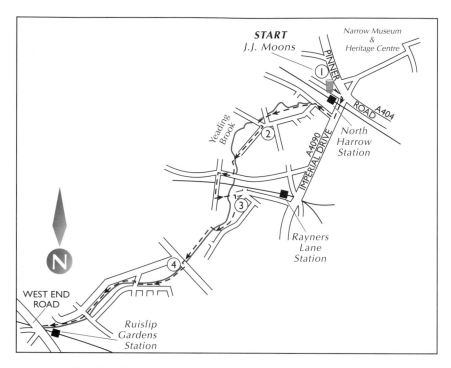

just grassland with trees including oak and ash. Leave via the metal gate. Turn right onto Village Way, the southern boundary of Harrow Garden Village. At the end, turn left onto Cannon Lane. Cross the Metropolitan and Piccadilly Lines via the separate footbridge, then come down onto the level and turn left into the park through the gateway opposite a new housing development. Take the tarmac path across Roxbourne Park, and cross a footbridge over Yeading Brook.

3. Turn right to follow the gravel path by the brook. This area is quite wild and overgrown, especially on the left of the stream. Opposite, above the high right-hand bank, is an open recreation ground that then gives way to grassland (you may need to walk on it if the river is in flood). Cross a brick-walled bridge over a side stream and turn right to regain the left bank of Yeading Brook. Emerge from the narrow track onto open grassland. At the end of this, turn right to cross the brook into the park and continue to the left, following the stream, past a wooded area stiff with hawthorns. Keep by the row of trees on your left. Pass a small group of trees on the right and a bench on the left, then about 20 yards further on take the path on the left down to stream level. On the far bank are allotments, by the stream are hawthorn and oak, and to the right are brambles. This is an excellent wildlife habitat. The trees occasionally clear to give a view of the meandering stream. Part of the grass is kept mown to mark the path, which becomes gravel underfoot, then leaves the park.

4. Cross Field End Road, turn left to cross the stream, then right to enter the kissing gate. Walk along the pathway lined with mature trees, on the left of the stream, passing allotments on the left. Pass a footbridge but, when you come to a road, Queens Walk, cross the bridge and continue along through the narrow meadow on the right of the stream, passing a stand of fine tall poplars. Cross the next road, Victoria Road (the route of frequent 114 buses to Ruislip, or South Harrow and Harrow), keeping on the right of the stream. Continue past wooded areas and then through a break in a former hedge into a large open meadow. Head diagonally across the meadow, to leave by a gate to the left of a children's play area. Turn left onto West End Road, pass the pub on the right and go under the railway bridge to arrive at Ruislip Gardens station.

Places of Interest Nearby

Harrow Museum and Heritage Centre, at Headstone Manor, north end of Pinner View (signposted down Station Road from the Pinner Road roundabout near the start) is on a site whose history can be dated back to AD 825. The magnificent tithe barn which houses the museum was built in 1506. To check opening times (on Wednesday to Sunday and Bank Holiday Mondays) telephone: 020 8861 2626.

WALK 15

ICKENHAM MARSH, YEADING BROOK AND THE PINN

Ickenham Marsh is a fascinating wetland on the outer fringes of London. Two minor rivers then lead you past a variety of open space near Ruislip.

The pub at the start of the walk

Ickenham Marsh is a nature reserve with a wild, bleak beauty. Ponds occupied by stands of reeds and reed mace are fed by Yeading Brook. Being next to the clear space of RAF Northolt, the marsh gives an impression of open moorland, but is just at the fringe of the suburbs. The reserve, run by the London Wildlife Trust, is an excellent place for wildflowers, especially dog roses, as well as insects and wildfowl. In early autumn, it's also a good source of blackberries.

The whole walk is very rewarding in autumn, as the trees alongside Yeading Brook, and later the Pinn, start turning a variety of hues and drop golden leaves into the water. This part of the course of the Pinn was once owned by King's College, Cambridge, and the walk passes through meadows near Ruislip still called Kings College Fields. As well as parks and woods to complete the circle, the walk takes you at one point through an unlit, curving tunnel under a railway line – bring a torch for this.

The Coach and Horses occupies a key position in the traditional centre of Ickenham on High Road, near the green, village pump, pond and church. At least part of the building dates from 1790, and inside there are low ceilings and wood panelling to give an antique ambience. Children are welcome in the dining area – food is available from 12 noon until 10 pm seven days a week, with a wide choice of starters, main meals and desserts, as well as lighter meals, jacket potatoes and baguettes, vegetarians are also catered for. Old Speckled Hen, Burton Ale, Marston's Pedigree and Tetley Bitter are the ales on draught, and wines and lagers are available. In good weather you can enjoy the large and pleasant garden, with play area. Telephone: 01895 623559.

- **HOW TO GET THERE:** The pub is on High Road, the B466, in the centre of Ickenham, not far from Hillingdon Circus on the A40. Underground: Ickenham (Piccadilly and Metropolitan Lines); the walk passes Ruislip Gardens (Central Line) at point 3.
- **PARKING:** There is a little space near the pub; Manor Farm (near Ruislip church, south of point 6) has car parks.
- **LENGTH OF THE WALK:** 6¾ miles. Map: OS Explorer 172 (mainly) and (some) 173 (GR 080862).

THE WALK

1. Leave the pub and turn right onto the main road, passing the village pump and pond. Turn right down Austin's Lane and continue over the tube line alongside woodland. At the end of Austin's Lane continue through a kissing gate and follow the Hillingdon Trail (HT) sign down a track next to a nature reserve. (Do not enter Glebe Avenue.) The route continues through pleasant woodland into Ickenham Marsh. Take the right fork near the noticeboard and continue to Yeading Brook.

2. Just before the footbridge (ignore the map and footpath sign), take the path to the left, so that the brook is on your right. Follow the path round to the left and right through the woods as it returns to the brook.

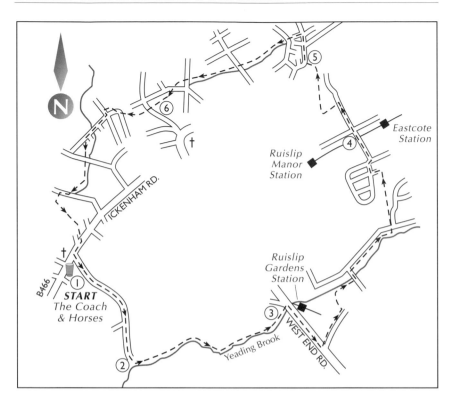

Follow the main path through trees, keeping the brook and aerodrome perimeter fence on the right. Come out of the woods onto a broader grass path. The grass broadens into a meadow on the left, but keep to the path with the brook on your right. Pass a footpath sign and continue down a gravel path through a garden area. Turn right onto West End Road.

3. Cross the road at the pelican crossing, turn right in front of Ruislip Gardens station, and then left into Bridgewater Road. Go under the tube line and turn left at the meadow. Walk down to Yeading Brook, turn right and follow the brook. At the road turn left, cross the stream and turn right to follow the brook, or, if muddy, the path by the garages. Pass some brookside poplars, then at the end of the garages turn left into the alleyway and continue straight over the road into Bessingby Fields. Keep to the tarmac path on the right of this popular open space, then pass a group of willows into the next field, Pine Gardens; the path is now on the left of the grassland, then becomes a broad concrete track. Follow this through the park to the gate onto Springfield Gardens. Turn left and then right at Coombe Drive. At the end turn right then immediatcly left into Oak Grove. Continue over the underground lines to the busy Elm Avenue.

4. Cross this road carefully and continue ahead along Lime Grove. Pass the ends of Acacia Avenue and Myrtle Avenue, then turn left through the gates into Warrender Park. Turn right into the park proper, then left towards the group of poplars. Turn right down the avenue of mature oaks. At the end, just to the right of a disused pond or sandpit, go through a break in the hedge, leading to woods. Follow the obvious path (which may be muddy) straight through, past a line of chestnut trees. Continue downhill to the more densely wooded area. At the bottom take the right fork and pass an overgrown pond. Continue straight on through the woods, climbing again. Pass a couple of numbered stakes (12 and 11) and continue on round to the left to pass 10, then keep on the main path through the centre of the wood, passing 9. Continue along the main path, bypassing some numbered stakes beside a clogged ditch, then take the first left to the water-filled ditch, then turn right to follow it past stake 4. On the right is a gravel path – take this and pass 3 to come to 2 just after on the main gravel path. Turn left at this main path (by 2) and continue straight on to the drive at the end. Turn left onto the drive and walk down to the main road.

5. At Eastcote Road, turn right, cross, then take the first left into Fore Street. Cross the bridge over the Pinn, then turn left onto a tarmac public footpath following the river; the overgrown tree-lined banks are a wild habitat. Cross over the next road, keeping to the right of the river, and enter the grassy meadow. Follow the possibly muddy path by the Pinn, noting the abundance of waterfowl here. Pass the end of the shrubbery and trees. On the right are playing fields; to the left, over the Pinn, is a floodlit games area. Follow the grass path away from the riverside towards an opening in the hedge by a large oak. Leave the meadow by the gateway. Cross Kings College Road, turn right, pass a pair of gates and a boarded-up pavilion, then turn left onto a drive, following the public footpath sign. Walk to the left of the pitch in front, just to the right of the low fence. At the end of the playing field turn left to go right of the fence into a meadow, then walk back down to the Pinn. At the next road leave via the metal gate on the right of the bridge. Cross the road, turn left to cross the bridge, then turn right to follow the left bank of the river. Follow the path across a small meadow to the main road, Pinn Way. Cross this road and enter the meadows on your left just before the bridge wall and walk along with the Pinn on your right. At the next road, Bury Street, go through the hedge onto a footpath. Turn right towards the bridge, but cross the road before the bridge and turn left through the gate into Kings Gardens.

6. The Pinn is on the right and there is a pond on your left; follow the tarmac path through the gardens, with streetlights and fine trees. Where the path turns left, turn right over a footbridge, then turn left onto a grass path with the Pinn's overgrown banks on the left and shrubs on the right. At the footbridge at the end turn left to cross it, then take the first right into Woodville Gardens. At the end, go through the barrier into the London Borough of Hillingdon meadow. The Pinn flows at the bottom right of the meadow, but keep to the obvious path along the top and enter the narrow footpath through the woods. Take the public footpath straight across the golf course – take care – and through the woods opposite (by a ditch). Leave the wood and cross a track (Clack Lane) then re-enter the golf course following HT markers; keep to the path. At the other side cross a plank bridge and keep to the right of the ditch, still following HT markers. Go through a wood and straight over another part of the golf course, heading for the noticeboard and gate opposite. Go over a plank bridge and exit through the gate. Go under the railway line through the dark tunnel (originally built for cattle) which veers to the left. Come to the road, turn right (HT signpost) and after about 35 yards turn left, following the HT sign into the alleyway. At the end of the alley turn left, following the HT sign onto a tree-lined grass track. Follow this old track, taking a left fork to cross a brick bridge over a stream, and come to the main road at the end next to the Soldier's Return pub. Turn right at the main road (HT sign) just after Parkfield Road, cross at the island (HT sign) and continue on the left-hand side of the road to return to the pub.

PLACES OF INTEREST NEARBY
Manor Farm in Ruislip, off Bury Lane opposite the church, has a group of old barns, which stand in the grounds of a former Norman castle. The great barn, possibly dating back to the 13th century, is a magnificent sight.

THE GRAND UNION CANAL AND DENHAM COUNTRY PARK

This walk is in one of the Colne valley's most attractive areas. You walk along a rural stretch of the Grand Union Canal towpath to Denham Lock, from where you enter the Denham Country Park Nature Reserve. From here you continue to charming Denham village. The return route is along woodland paths.

Widewater Lock

The Denham Country Park Nature Reserve was opened in 1992. It comprises 70 acres of woodland and wetland and is bounded by the Grand Union Canal and the Misbourne and Colne rivers. The woodlands are home to many species of songbirds, and in summer damselflies and dragonflies can be seen in the wetland areas. Within the park is the Colne Valley Park Visitor Centre.

The walk begins at the Horse and Barge pub overlooking the canal at Moorhall Road, South Harefield. There is a pleasant conservatory

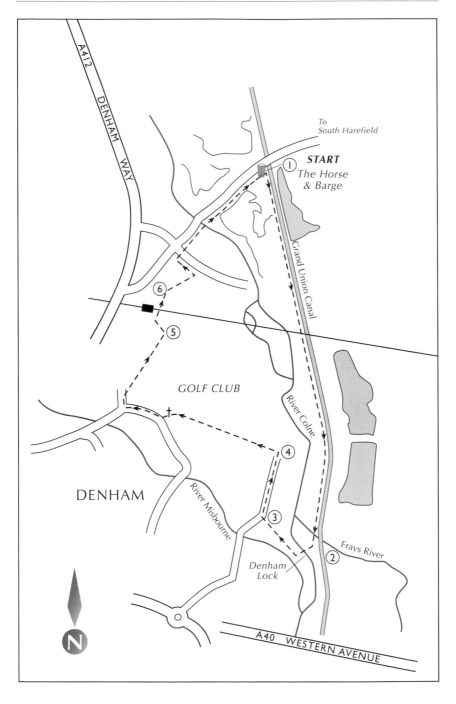

restaurant in this friendly, family pub and a large garden with a children's playground. A comprehensive menu includes sirloin steak, fish dishes, chicken and steak and kidney pie. Beers include Courage Best and Directors, John Smith's Smooth and Guinness. The pub keeps all-day hours, from 11 am on Monday to Saturday and from 12 noon on Sundays. Telephone: 01895 834080.

- **HOW TO GET THERE:** From Denham Roundabout on the A40 take the A412 to Denham and turn right onto Moorfield Road. The pub is on the south side of Moorhall Road, an easterly continuation of Moorfield Road. Rail: Denham station (trains hourly from Marylebone) is on the walk route. Underground: Northwood (Metropolitan Line) and then the 331 bus to Moorhall Road.
- **PARKING:** There is a car park just off Moorhall Road on the south-east side of the canal. Alternatively, you could park at the Colne Valley Park Visitor Centre (point 3).
- **LENGTH OF THE WALK:** 3½ miles. Map: OS Explorer 172 (GR 050887).

THE WALK

1. Start off on the west side of the towpath by the pub, going south. This is a beautiful rural stretch of canal with many houseboats. Continue ahead to Denham Lock, the deepest on the canal. Its great depth was necessary to take the canal over the man-made Frays River. Opposite is Denham Quarry, one of several flooded gravel pits in the area that are now recreational lakes and wildlife refuges.

2. Just beyond the lock, by a Denham Country Park notice, turn right onto the South Bucks Way Path. Cross the footbridge over the River Colne and continue along the path. Go through the wooden gate and continue ahead, passing Misbourne Meadow on the right. In the meadow, near the fence, is a row of anthills. The hills took many years to develop and the soil within them is constantly being overturned by the ants with the result that plants which favour well-aerated and well-drained ground flourish here. Go through another gate and continue along the path. At the four-ways signpost and crosspaths continue ahead, following the South Bucks Way sign.

3. Go through the kissing gate. If you wish to visit the Colne Valley Park Visitor Centre, cross the approach road to the golf course, go through another kissing gate and continue ahead to the centre on the left. Otherwise turn right onto this approach road to enter the grounds of the golf course.

4. Pass a white bridge on the right, and opposite the second white bridge, which leads to the club house entrance, turn left onto a tarmac track, signposted 'public footpath'. Continue ahead along this long, straight avenue of trees. Go through the kissing gate and large wrought iron gate, cross over the road and go through the gate into the grounds of St Mary's church. Walk around the church and leave the grounds by the lychgate. Turn right onto Village Road and continue ahead into Denham village. When Village Road veers left, continue straight ahead on the road to the right of the village green. Pass Denham Place on the left and follow the road as it turns right and becomes the Pyghtle. Continue ahead when it narrows to a tree-fringed tarmac track to the left of the golf course.

5. Continue ahead, keeping on the tarmac path when it turns left beside two dirt paths, and then veers right to pass the steps up to Denham station on the left.

6. At the wide fork turn right to continue on a tarmac path flanked by high hedges. In spring look out for songbirds which nest here. At the end of the path turn left onto Savay Lane and at the T-junction turn right onto Moorfield Road and continue ahead to reach the pub.

PLACES OF INTEREST NEARBY
The *Colne Valley Park Visitor Centre* in Denham Country Park is open from April to October. There is a café and a shop. In the grounds are picnic benches and a children's adventure playground. To check opening times, telephone: 01895 833375.

HAREFIELD, THE GRAND UNION CANAL AND SEVERAL LAKES

❧❀❧

Starting by the Grand Union Canal at Coppermill Lock in Harefield, you walk along the towpath to Rickmansworth, where you can visit the Batchworth Lock Canal Centre. The route continues through woodland, passing four of a series of lakes created from disused gravel pits, before returning along the canal towpath.

Springwell Lake

This stretch of the Grand Union Canal is part of the Colne Valley Park and although rich in industrial history it is now almost entirely rural, passing a number of important habitats for flora and fauna.

Gravel was extracted in this area for twenty years, and when work was completed in the 1950s the area was flooded. Most of the lakes thus formed are important wildlife habitats, but Batchworth and Bury Lakes, passed on the walk, are now recreational, and comprise the Rickmansworth Aquadrome.

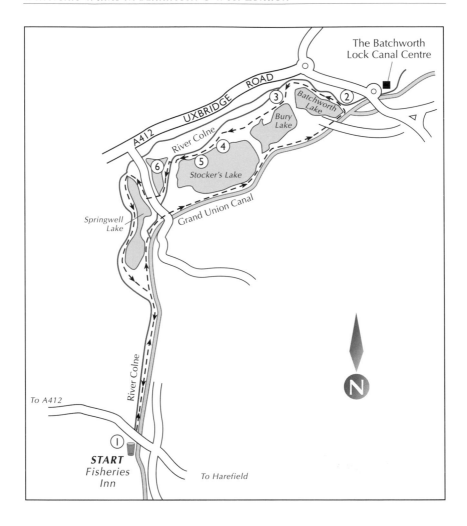

The walk begins at the Fisheries Inn which enjoys a superb setting between the canal and the River Colne at Coppermill Lock. It has a spacious bar, restaurant and riverside garden. The extensive menu includes fish, vegetarian and steak dishes and a good choice of starters and desserts. Food is served Monday to Thursday 12 noon to 3pm and 7.30pm to 9pm; Friday and Saturday 10am to 3pm and 5.30pm to 10pm; Sunday 12 noon to 6.30pm. Tetley's Bitter, Pedigree Bitter and Old Speckled Hen are the beers. Children are welcome in the restaurant and garden. Telephone: 01895 82623.

- **HOW TO GET THERE:** Leave the A40 at Uxbridge Circus onto the B467 north, then turn left at the roundabout, onto Harvil Road. Underground: Either Northwood (Metropolitan Line) then bus 331, or Rickmansworth (Metropolitan Line) from where you could start the walk (joining the route in point 2).
- **PARKING:** There is a large pub car park but please ask before leaving your car whilst you walk. There is also parking at Springwell Lake just off Springwell Lane (point 6).
- **LENGTH OF THE WALK:** 6 miles. Map: OS Explorer 172 (GR 040912).

The Walk

1. Leave the pub and turn left onto the canal towpath. Pass Coppermill Lock where a sluice enables canoeists to practise white water rafting – a rare sight on a canal. The impressive, renovated brick buildings on the left were originally paper mills but converted into copper mills at the end of the 18th century. The copper was used to line the bottom of wooden long boats.

Keep going along the towpath, crossing the bridge over the River Colne, where longboats are moored in the adjacent Maplecross Basin. Continue ahead under the Springwell Lane bridge and pass the Springwell Reed Bed Nature Reserve. This large, undisturbed reed bed is an important habitat for a variety of water birds. On the opposite side of the canal is the weather-boarded Stocker's Farm which dates back to the 1500s. Go under the bridge at Stocker's Lock, named after the farm, and continue ahead towards Rickmansworth Bridge.

2. If you wish to visit the Batchworth Lock Canal Centre continue ahead under the bridge and the centre is on the left. Otherwise, just before a humpback bridge which carries the towpath over the River Colne, and opposite a large branch of Tesco on the right, turn left and go through the metal gates to enter the grounds of Rickmansworth Aquadrome, passing an information board on the left. Continue ahead on the track which skirts the north-eastern end of Batchworth Lake. Ignore the turn off right and continue ahead, passing Rickmansworth Waterski Club on the right. At the fork veer right to walk along a track through mixed woodland, to the left of the River Colne. Look out for signs indicating poplar and alder woods, a heron halt and dragonfly pond.

3. At the T-junction turn right onto a path to the right of Bury Lake. Continue ahead and go through a high metal gate. At the next T-junction turn right and continue to the footbridge over the River Colne, signposted to Mill End and Uxbridge Road.

4. Turn left just before the bridge, onto a narrow path signposted to Springwell and Inns Lakes. Continue ahead and go through a kissing gate to enter Stocker's Lake Nature Reserve. This lake has a number of islets acting as nesting sites and refuges for a variety of birds, including grebe. It is well screened by trees, with breaks to allow good viewing. Proceed ahead on this path.

5. By a wooden fence, turn left onto a narrow, ill-defined path which passes a heron viewpoint – the lake has the largest heronry in Hertfordshire. Cormorants can also be seen from here, fishing from perches in the lake. Maintain direction along this path to regain the main path. Continue ahead to a bridge over the river, adjacent to a picnic bench and a T-junction.

6. Turn right to cross the bridge, following a sign to Springwell and Inns Lakes. Continue to the end of this lakeside path and go through a kissing gate onto Springwell Lane. Cross over and take the path to the right of Springwell Lake car park. Go through a kissing gate and continue ahead, following a sign for the Springwell Lake Circular Walk. Follow this path through lush vegetation, to the right of the lake and left of the river, eventually reaching the board walk where the path has raised wooden ramps to prevent slipping. Keep on the path as it veers left to skirt the southern end of the lake. At the path's end continue along the tarmac. Just before the bridge, take the dirt path veering right. Go through the kissing gate and turn right onto the towpath to return to Coppermill Lock.

PLACES OF INTEREST NEARBY
The *Batchworth Lock Canal Centre* in Rickmansworth is the home of the restored traditional narrowboat *Roger*, one of the last wooden boats to carry coal on the canal. To check the centre's opening times, telephone: 01293 778382.

ARKLEY AND DOLLIS BROOK

*This is a mostly rural walk in an area with much to offer walkers,
evident by the plethora of waymarks you will pass along the route. After
crossing an open meadow with fine views, and taking a woodland path
past the grounds of Windmill House, the walk follows Dollis Brook
through meadows and woodland to Barnet, then returns to Arkley via
the gently sloping meadows of King George's Field.*

High Barnet

Arkley straddles the A411, just south-west of Barnet, near the site of
Watling Street, the Roman road which once linked London to the north-
west via Verulamium (present day St Albans). It continued to be a
major through route for traffic, and by the late 17th century around 150
coaches a day passed through, carrying the 'jet setters' of the times. All
this traffic placed a tremendous burden on the roads and from 1712
they were maintained by tolls. The posts from one tollgate remain and
can be seen on the walk.

    Arkley developed after the opening of East Barnet and High Barnet

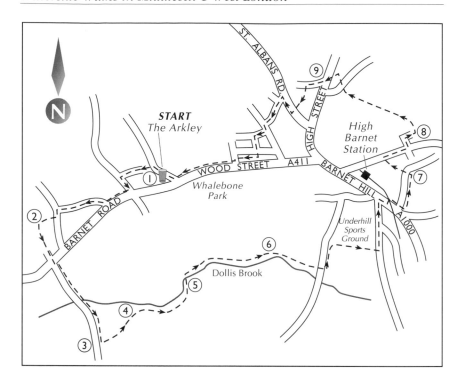

stations on the Great Northern Railway. The distinctive, well-preserved Arkley Windmill, dating from this time, is now in the private grounds of Windmill House but you glimpse it on the walk.

The walk begins at the Arkley, a popular, friendly pub on Barnet Road. It has plenty of comfortable seating areas where children can eat with their parents, and a children's menu. There is a conservatory restaurant, and dining tables on a shaded patio. Food is served every day at lunchtime and in the evening and all-day hours are kept, from 11 am on Monday to Saturday and 12 noon on Sunday (with the exception of Monday to Thursday during January, February and March when the pub closes in the afternoon). Ind Coope Burton Ale, Tetley Bitter and Benskins are stocked alongside a full range of bottled beers, lagers and wines. Telephone: 020 8449 3862.

- **HOW TO GET THERE:** Turn westwards off Barnet Hill (A1000) just south of the High Street onto Wood Street (A411) which becomes Barnet Road. Underground: Edgware or High Barnet (both Northern Line) then bus 107.

- **PARKING:** In the pub car park (please ask before leaving your car whilst you walk), or there is a small car park behind St Peter's church, opposite the war memorial at Rowley Green Road, near the beginning of the walk. There is also a car park at High Barnet station, which is close to the walk route.
- **LENGTH OF THE WALK:** 6½ miles. Map: OS Explorer 173 (GR 233964).

THE WALK

Note: Waymarks referred to along the route are DVGW (Dollis Valley Green Walk), LL (London Loop) and BCLW (Barnet Countryside Leisure Walks). Parts of this walk are along paths which are sometimes muddy in winter.

1. Leave the pub, turn left and left again to walk up Galley Lane. When the road curves right, turn left onto a bridlepath signposted 'Arkley Lane'. When the path ends continue ahead along Oaklands Lane. Turn left onto Arkley Lane and then immediately right onto Barnet Road.

At the war memorial turn right onto Rowley Green Road and continue ahead, crossing over to walk on the pavement. Turn left onto Rowley Lane and then right onto a footpath signposted to Ripon Way and Barnet Gate.

2. A little way along turn left across a stile marked with a yellow arrow. Follow the path across a meadow from where there are good views of Borehamwood and beyond. Go over another stile and continue ahead along a leafy path, shortly passing the grounds of Windmill House on the left. At the end of the path continue ahead, passing Hadley Football Club on the right.

At the T-junction turn right onto Barnet Road, cross over and pass the Gate pub, named after an adjacent tollgate, the posts of which remain. Turn left onto Hendon Wood Lane and continue ahead.

3. Just past the Old Choleleian Sports Ground, turn left through a kissing gate into Totteridge Fields, following DVGW and LL signs. Continue ahead on the path through two meadows, following DVGW, LL and BCLW signs. Keep on the path as it veers left at a T-junction, and then turns right at an LL sign to skirt the edge of a playing field.

4. About a quarter of the way around the field, veer right, still following the DVGW and LL arrows. Descend the steps and cross a wooden footbridge. Go through a kissing gate and veer left to follow the path alongside the tree-lined brook. Go through another kissing gate, still following LL and DVGW signs, and continue ahead on the path, ignoring a footbridge and stile on the left. Follow the path as it veers left and goes through yet another kissing gate. Proceed across the narrow part of a meadow, passing on the left, by shrubbery, a post with DVGW and LL signs. Continue ahead, keeping close to the shrubbery. Go through two metal kissing gates flanking a footbridge and press ahead, still with the brook on your left. After going through another two metal kissing gates flanking a footbridge, keep on the path to go through a wooden kissing gate by a metal gate, still following DVGW and LL signs.

Follow the path diagonally across the field and cross the wooden footbridge. Continue ahead through a meadow with pylons, keeping near the tree-lined brook on the left.

5. At the three-way green sign, go through the kissing gate and over the footbridge, then turn right, still following the waymarks. The brook is now on your right. Continue ahead, cross a wide stretch of tarmac and go through the gap in the fence.

6. Just before a footbridge, turn right and then left over a stile. Continue ahead, either on the grass or the parallel tarmac path to the left. At the crosspaths, by another footbridge and a three-way sign, continue ahead on the tarmac path. After passing allotments and a housing estate on the left bear right at the fork, following a DVGW sign. At Barnet Lane turn left and continue ahead.

At the pedestrian lights turn right onto the tarmac track between Underhill Sports Ground and Barnet Playing Fields. Continue ahead to Grasvenor Avenue, passing a play area on the left. Turn left and continue ahead, following the LL signpost and maintaining direction along Fairfield Way. Turn right at Barnet Hill and go under the bridge. Cross over at the pedestrian lights, and turn right and immediately left onto Potters Lane, following an LL sign.

7. After the road curves, follow an LL sign to turn left and go down a path to a field. Veer right to follow the path around the perimeter. Pass the end of Kingsmead, and at Meadway turn right and continue ahead.

Cross over and turn left onto Burnside Close. Follow the road as it veers right, and then maintain direction along the cycle track.

8. Turn left through the kissing gate into King George's Field, and continue ahead, following an LL sign and staying on the path when it veers slightly left at the end of the first meadow. At the second and third meadows continue ahead and slightly uphill, still following an LL sign. At the top of the third meadow there's a bench on which you can sit and enjoy the good views of Barnet and beyond. Near the bench is another LL sign which you follow to go through a kissing gate onto Hadley Green (the road). Cross over and walk halfway around the pond to cross the High Street at the traffic island.

9. Turn left, and immediately right onto Christ Church Lane. After passing the end of Gladsmuir Road, continue ahead along the tarmac track, and at the T-junction turn left onto Christchurch Passage footpath. At St Albans Road turn right, cross over, and turn left onto Alston Road. Just before the road curves left, and where Alston Road becomes The Avenue, cross over the road at the traffic island, then cross Wentworth Road to turn right onto Marriot Road. Turn left onto Ravenscroft Park, continue ahead and cross over at the T-junction. Go through the metal gate and down the wooden steps into the public garden sandwiched between Ravenscroft Park and busy Wood Street. Turn sharp right and walk along the tarmac path to leave the garden through another metal gate. Turn left onto Blenheim Road and then right onto Wood Street to return to the pub.

PLACES OF INTEREST NEARBY
The Bull Arts Centre, 68 High Street, Barnet, holds exhibitions of contemporary painting, sculpture and photography. Telephone: 020 8449 0048.

Barnet Museum, 31 Wood Street, tells the history of the area from the Battle of Barnet to the present day. Entry is free. Telephone: 020 8440 8066.

TOTTERIDGE AND DOLLIS BROOK

This pretty, rural circuit begins in Totteridge. After passing the tree-fringed pond at the southern end of Totteridge Green, you walk across meadowland and then along a leafy bridleway. The route continues through woodland and managed parkland on a section of the Dollis Valley Green Walk, and you will be alongside the brook for over half the walk.

Dollis Brook

Totteridge is especially favoured, as parts of it seem deep in the country, yet the Northern Line to central London is close at hand. There was a hamlet here as early as the 13th century. Like Arkley, featured in Walk 18, Totteridge grew after the opening of the Barnet stations on the Great Northern Railway.

The walk starts at the Orange Tree pub on Totteridge Village (the road). The present building dates from the 1800s and has a picturesque site set back from the road behind a pond fringed by trees. Inside there is a comfortable lounge bar and a separate restaurant. Children accompanied by adults are allowed in both until 9 pm. Filled baguettes can be obtained all day in the bar; the restaurant is open at lunchtime and in the evening. The beers on handpump are Charrington IPA, Worthington Best Bitter and Fuller's London Pride. Telephone: 020 8343 6961.

- **HOW TO GET THERE:** Totteridge Village (road) is the A5109, leaving the A1000 at Whetstone, and the pub is just beyond Totteridge Green, past the school, on the left. Underground: Totteridge and Whetstone (Northern Line). Part of the walk (point 6) passes close to the station. Buses: Route 251 (Monday to Saturday) Arnos Grove-Stanmore passes the pub.
- **PARKING:** On the pub approach drive (this can get busy). Otherwise try the side streets around the green.
- **LENGTH OF THE WALK:** 6 miles. Map: OS Explorer 173 (GR 248939).

THE WALK

1. From the bus stop outside the Orange Tree pub, walk away from the main road, and just before The Close turn left onto a tarmac track. Continue ahead, passing the back of the pub on the left and several houses and the Consolata Missionary College on the right. Continue along the path as it bears slightly right.

At the pond veer right and keep right to walk along a fenced path. Go over the stile, and then shortly over another stile. Cross a footbridge over a brook, go over another stile and continue ahead to a stile on the right.

2. Cross this stile and keep going till eventually you reach a kissing gate.

3. Once through the kissing gate turn left onto a shrubbery-fringed bridleway. Continue to Partingdale Lane, turn left and proceed to the junction with Lullington Garth/Frith Lane where you turn right and walk ahead along the pavement.

4. After passing the entrance to West Linton Close on the left, turn left onto the pine-fringed approach to Finchley Golf Club. When the road veers right, continue straight ahead to a bridge over Dollis Brook.
5. Do not cross, but turn left at the bridge, to walk along the pretty

89

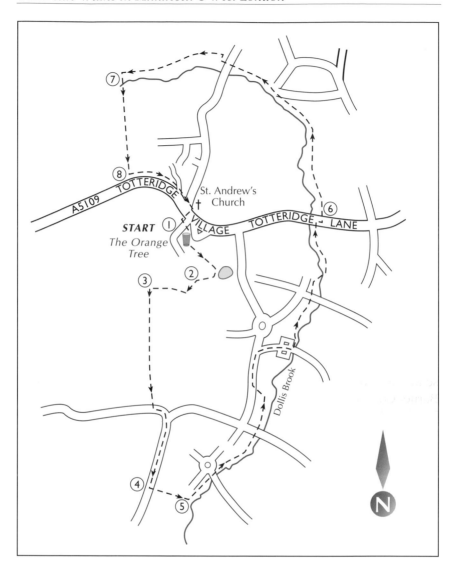

tree-lined path skirting the brook. This is part of the Dollis Valley Green Walk. Continue to Fursby Avenue, cross over and continue ahead through parkland, passing a footbridge on the right and the Riverside Walk Play Area on the left. Cross over Lullington Garth/Argyle Road and continue on the riverside path, passing another footbridge on the right.

At Southover Way turn right, continue ahead and take the first right onto Tillingham Way. Proceed along here and when the road curves right, turn left to regain the Dollis Valley Green Walk, still to the left of the brook. Continue ahead, cross over Laurel Way, go through the metal gate and proceed ahead along the tarmac track, still following the brook through parkland. Keep on the path when it crosses to the right side of the brook. At Totteridge Lane turn right and cross over at the traffic island.

6. Turn left just before the houses, to regain the Dollis Valley Green Walk on a tarmac path running to the right of a cycle track. Continue ahead through parkland, with the tree-fringed winding brook down to the left. Pass the end of Western Way and continue along the path as it veers right. At the T-junction bordering Barnet Playing Fields, turn left to continue ahead, following the brook and a Dollis Valley Green Walk sign. At the end of the sports field continue ahead, following the three-way signpost. At Barnet Lane turn right, in order to cross over the road at the traffic island, and turn left to follow the London Loop Walk sign. The brook is still on your left.

7. At the crosspaths turn left to follow a Yellow Circular Walk sign. Cross over the bridge and proceed along the tarmac path, passing a school and playing field on the left. Then continue ahead following a Barnet Countryside Leisure Walks sign. Cross over the end of Oaklands Road and continue ahead, crossing the drive to Oaklands (a house). Go through a kissing gate and continue ahead on a grassy track.

8. At the main road turn left and continue ahead. Cross over Barnet Lane, pass the war memorial on the left and continue to St Andrew's church. Enter the churchyard through the lychgate and walk towards the church, passing a huge yew tree, over 1,000 years old, on the right. After having a look around the church (Pepys family connections) and churchyard leave by the lychgate and turn left. Cross to the right side of the road to return to the pub.

PLACES OF INTEREST NEARBY
The Jewish Museum at 80 East End Road (part of the A504) in Finchley houses a large social history collection reflecting the diverse roots and heritage of Jews in Britain. Admission charge. For opening times, telephone: 020 8349 1143.

THE (OLD) NEW RIVER AND TURKEY BROOK AT ENFIELD

This walk leads you through the charming historic centre of Enfield and the grounds of Forty Hall along a route established by a pioneer of water supply.

The New River (old course)

This walk is dominated by the New River, a watercourse constructed in 1609-1613 by Sir Hugh Myddleton to supply water to Clerkenwell from springs near Ware. His original watercourse has been bypassed over the centuries, and is now shown on maps as 'New River (Old Course)'. The New Course, of course, has supposedly now been made redundant by the new Ring Main. Myddleton's New River is now a meandering backwater that determines the appearance of the centre of Enfield and flows through the wilder surroundings of Forty Hall. Turkey Brook is another stream providing a pleasant walking route through these grounds.

The Crown and Horseshoes occupies a wonderful position right next to the old course of the New River in old Enfield. The pub is open all day every day, and the freshly cooked food is a strong point. You can enjoy anything from a snack up to a three-course meal, including an all-day breakfast and Sunday roasts (food only until 5 pm on Sundays). A couple of tables indoors, and one side of the large tree-filled garden overlook the river. Beers served include Boddingtons Bitter, Fuller's London Pride, Caledonian 80/- and a guest. Telephone: 020 8363 1371.

- **HOW TO GET THERE:** The A110 passes through the centre of Enfield; the pub is near Cricketers Arms Road off Chase Side (left just before Church Street bridge heading east). Rail: Enfield Town or Enfield Chase, then walk to Church Street and follow the river north. The walk passes near Turkey Street (at the start of point 4) and Southbury (in point 6, turn left at Southbury Road).
- **PARKING:** Very little near the pub. There is ample parking at Forty Hall (point 4).
- **LENGTH OF THE WALK:** 7½ miles. Map: OS Explorer 173 (GR 324970).

THE WALK

1. Leave the pub and turn right along the path by the New River. Turn left at the first footbridge and take the road by the river. Follow the footpath round to the right, opposite the playing field on the other bank. Leave the river at a footpath on the left which comes out on Parsonage Lane. Cross the road, go straight into Monastery Gardens opposite and follow this round to the right as far as Baker Street.

2. Turn left, walk down to Cheviot Close on the left, cross over and walk down the public footpath opposite, just before the Emmanuel Centre. At the end of the footpath turn left onto Churchbury Lane. Pass Chace Community School; at the end, cross Canonbury Road, keep straight on down the alleyway and turn right to follow a footpath, emerging into Middleton Avenue, just opposite Hallside Road. Cross Middleton Avenue, turn left and follow it to the roundabout. Just after 1 Forty Hill, turn right into the road barred to traffic, go past iron gates, then turn left onto a gravel public footpath just before the first house. This substantial path leads through quite wild broad-leaf woodland, with the old course of the New River on your left. Keep left through woods at a riverside signpost (Mile and a Quarter footpath) near the

93

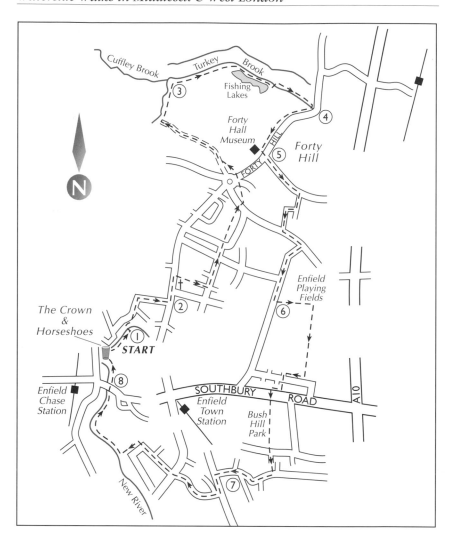

entrance to Forty Hall, staying on the right side of the New River.

3. At a crossroads and signpost, turn sharp right on Mile and a Quarter footpath towards Forty Hall Fishing Lakes and Whitewebbs Lane, on the right of Turkey Brook. A bridleway is on the left, but keep to the footpath. Ignore a gate and concrete bridge over the brook, staying on a broad gravel path through woods with the brook on the left. Keep straight on, following London Loop signs, ignoring a fork to the right and a footbridge. You have water on both sides – Turkey Brook on the left and the lake on the right. As you pass the second fishing lake, look to the right up a line of trees in the meadow to see Forty Hall. Keep a lookout on the left, however: just before a metal gate in the hedge on the right turn left to take a wooden footbridge over the stream, then turn right to follow the stream on your right. Just before the brick road bridge, turn right to recross the stream on a wooden footbridge.

4. Now walk back, along the perimeter of a field. The path goes partly through woods, then uphill through parkland with fine planted trees. Walk straight across a car park and exit by the main metal gate. Cross the main drive (main gates on left) and walk down a gravel path between trees, roughly following the perimeter of the grounds. Pass a bench commemorating two of the gardeners, and leave at the next exit (a kissing gate) on the left, opposite Forty Hill House.

5. Turn right past the end of the driveway, cross the road and take the first turning left, Goat Lane. Turn right onto Garnault Road, follow it to the right at the end (not down Chinnery Close), then go left into Layard Road. At Carterhatch Lane, turn left opposite the entrance to the Jewish Cemetery. Cross the bridge over the New River, then turn right onto Ladysmith Road (a footpath cuts off the corner). Follow the road round to the left. Go through a traffic gate (crossing a path that leads to a footbridge on the right) and keep straight on down the avenue.

6. Just after no 217, turn left onto a footpath, follow it along the side of the recreation ground and enter Enfield Playing Fields by the gateway on the right. Walk down the central avenue of chestnut trees and leave by the main exit at the far end, just to the right of the sports field. Turn right onto Sketty Road, then left into Clydach Road and at the main Southbury Road turn right. Cross at the pelican crossing just before the school. Immediately opposite is the entrance to Bush Hill Park, which closes at sunset. Go through the metal gates and walk down the chestnut avenue. At the end leave through the gate and turn right. Take the path at the end of the block of flats (signposted 'Library') before James Street, passing garages and a road joining at the left, then exit at Agricola Place onto Main Avenue between two churches. Turn right down tree-lined Main Avenue and continue round to the right into East Crescent. At the end, turn right to cross the railway line by the footbridge.

7. At the other side, take the left path away from the railway into tree-lined Abbey Road and keep straight on to Wellington Road. Cross over and turn left onto this lime avenue. Take first right onto a road that's actually named Private Road. Cross Village Road and, at the end of Private Road, turn left (you'll see a brick wall hiding the entrance of the New River into an underground culvert) and then immediately right into Walsingham Road. At the end of Walsingham Road continue down the footpath to the park. In Town Park turn left and walk down the grass to the left of the tennis courts to reach the New River (old course) which bounds the park. Turn right to walk along the path by the bank. At the end of the park, leave the park by the gate but turn right before the footbridge to follow the riverside path past the island in the New River.

8. At Church Street bridge over the river, cross the main road and go straight down Gentleman's Row to the left of Trinity church. Cross the river by the footbridge at the end of the green and turn right down River View by the watercourse back to the pub.

PLACES OF INTEREST NEARBY
The walk passes through the grounds of *Forty Hall*, built in 1632, which houses a museum. Telephone: 020 8363 9495.